Dead are all gods. Now we want the overman to live.[1]

Bibliographic Information held by the German National Library: The details of the original German edition of this publication are held by the German National Library as part of the German National Bibliography; detailed bibliographical data can be found online at www.dnb.de.

© 2018 Dr Walther Ziegler
1st Edition June 2018
Jacket design and graphic design for the whole book: Silke Ruthenberg, making use of illustrations by:
Raphael Bräsecke, Creactive – Studio for Advertising, Comics & Illustrations
© JackF - Fotolia.com (image-frames)
© Valerie Potapova - Fotolia.com (image-frames)
© Svetlana Gryankina - Fotolia.com (speech-balloons)

Publisher and Printing:
BoD – Books on Demand, Norderstedt
ISBN 9783752803822

Walther Ziegler

Nietzsche

in 60 Minutes

Translated by
Alexander Reynolds

My thanks go to Rudolf Aichner for his tireless critical editing; Silke Ruthenberg for the fine graphics; Lydia Pointvogl, Eva Amberger, Christiane Hüttner, and Dr. Martin Engler for their excellent work as manuscript readers and sub-editors; Prof. Guntram Knapp, who first inspired me with enthusiasm for philosophy; and Angela Schumitz, who handled in the most professional manner, as chief editorial reader, the production of both the German and the English editions of this series of books.

My special thanks go to my translator

Dr Alexander Reynolds.

Himself a philosopher, he not only translated the original German text into English with great care and precision but also, in passages where this was required in order to ensure clear understanding, supplemented this text with certain formulations adapted specifically to the needs of English-language readers.

Contents

Nietzsche's Great Discovery

Friedrich Nietzsche (1844-1900) has the reputation of being the darkest, most radical and most controversial of all philosophers. The darkest because he was deeply sceptical of all that had hitherto given solace, moral security and hope to human beings; the most radical because he dared to tear up by the roots all that had seemed, for centuries, most valid and most permanent; and the most controversial because his provocative philosophy has, even today, as many rancorous critics as it has passionate adherents.

Nietzsche's work is more than just a milestone in the history of philosophy. It is like a flash of summer lightning, a sea-change in humankind's own perception of itself. Its core idea has imbedded itself deep in modern consciousness. In just one short sentence he enunciated what has remained the abiding problem of all Western civilization right up to the present day:

God is dead![2]

The phrase is known all around the world, even to those who know nothing of Nietzsche. Because with it Nietzsche gives concise expression to a feeling that seized humankind in the age that saw the rise of the natural sciences and has not let go of us since. It is a feeling that culminates in the atheism prevalent in modern mass society and forces us to pose entirely anew the question of what sense and meaning our lives can have. But this "death of God" that Nietzsche proclaims in his *magnum opus* of 1885, *Thus Spoke Zarathustra*, is not a single event but rather a process which throws its own shadows ahead of it:

What I relate is the history of the next two centuries. I describe what is coming, what can no longer come differently: *the advent of nihilism.* [3]

For almost two thousand years Christianity seemed able to explain the whole nature of the world; for the same long period human beings could feel secure in the sense of being God's creatures. Nietzsche was one of the first to sense that this old worldpicture was about to suffer an irrevocable collapse.

Nietzsche's contemporary Darwin had just recently developed his theory of evolution, according to which Man was no creature of God but just a higher mammal. Marx, around this time, was exhorting humanity to finally take its destiny into its own hands. Physics, medicine and the other natural sciences, meanwhile, were going from strength to strength. All that was not scientifically provable was called into question: divine creation; immaculate conception; finally, even God Himself. But it was not just scientists and researchers, Nietzsche argues, but all of us together who gradually took away from God His world-explaining power:

Where is God? *We have killed him* – you and I! We are all his murderers. [4]

Nietzsche calls himself an "immoralist" and an "anti-Christian". On one possible English rendering of the title of one of his major late works, he even goes so far to calls himself "the Antichrist". But his core idea consists in more than just a critique of Christianity and morality. Rather, he is interested above all in one question: how is humankind to go on if that belief in a "beyond" which had sustained us is doomed to lose all force in the two centuries to come? What happens when nihilism gains the ascendancy and the spiritual shelter provided by religion is irrecoverably lost?

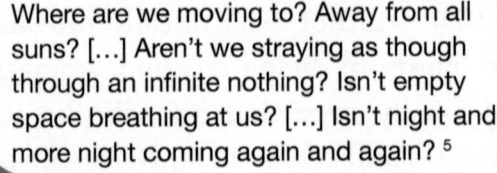

Where are we moving to? Away from all suns? [...] Aren't we straying as though through an infinite nothing? Isn't empty space breathing at us? [...] Isn't night and more night coming again and again? [5]

What Nietzsche poses here is the great question of identity in the age of "the advent of nihilism". With the "death of God" such principles as the Ten Commandments, piety and humility also lose their power to order and structure our world. Are there any values left, then, that are worth living and dying for?

It is because this question is such a burningly topical one that Nietzsche is often called the first "post-modern" thinker. Why "post-modern"? The modern age was still sustained by the optimism and the expectation of progress of the Enlightenment. Such thinkers as Rousseau, Voltaire, Montesquieu, Kant, Locke and Hume had already aspired to free humankind of superstition and religious humility. But Nietzsche is more radical. He goes one large step farther and asks: what is to happen once we have freed ourselves of these things? Once all mythical and religious world-images have been destroyed, what is it that still gives life meaning? His answer is a rigorously consistent one:

Since the belief has ceased that a God broadly directs the destinies of the world [...] Man has to set himself ecumenical goals embracing the whole earth [...] Herein lies the tremendous task. [6]

We have, then, the "tremendous task" of setting for ourselves those goals which shall, in future, be pursued across the whole earth. This is the great freedom that has become ours after "the death of God". But – so Nietzsche argues – instead of becoming aware of this freedom and making use of it, we human beings have immediately set about making for ourselves new gods, new idols, which promise us the shelter and directing force we have lost. The "small-minded" – so Nietzsche's prognosis – will turn, in lieu of the divine, to hundreds of thousands of more material promises of salvation. He saw the future as one in which people would run blindly after nationalism, socialism, racism or the supposed "blessings" of modern capitalism and democracy. Nietzsche's critique of this new "idolatry" is astonishingly far-sighted. As a convinced European he was particularly irked by the idolization of "Germanness" common among his contemparies and indeed by all forms of nationalism:

Is there any idea at all behind this bovine nationalism? What value can there be now, when everything points to wider and more common interests, in encouraging this boorish self-conceit? [7]

Besides the "bovine" nationalists there are also many "sheep", who replace the old religion with a leader whom they can blindly follow:

The poor sheep say to their shepherd: "go on ahead and we shall never lack the courage to follow you". The poor shepherd, however, thinks to himself: "follow me, and I shall never lack the courage to lead you." [8]

Nietzsche describes the masses who trot along, in this way, after a leader who has arisen from their midst as being like arithmetical "zeros":

[...] You want to multiply yourself by ten, by a hundred? You are looking for disciples? Look for *zeros*!" [9]

Anti-Semitism too Nietzsche saw as an attempt by the "small-minded" to give meaning to their lives, an illusory elevation of their own existences:

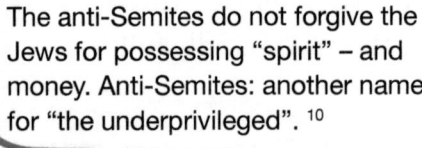

The anti-Semites do not forgive the Jews for possessing "spirit" – and money. Anti-Semites: another name for "the underprivileged". [10]

There is in Germany no more shameless and stupid a gang than these anti-Semites. [11]

There can, then, be no doubt. Nietzsche was many things, but he was not a Nazi. The only thing that Hitler can genuinely be said to have "taken over" from Nietzsche was his walking stick, which Nietzsche's sister, Elisabeth Foerster-Nietzsche, gave to the dictator as a gift many years after the philosopher's death. As for Nietzsche's writings, Hitler never read a word of them.

But just as Nietzsche condemned nationalism and anti-Semitism, he also saw a great danger in socialism. For socialism too is a new "promise of salvation" offered to those who feel themselves uprooted and unguided after "the death of God". At the end of this path, however, lies not any promised redemption through a "worker's paradise" but rather the suppression of all individuality:

[Socialism] desires an abundance of state power such as only despotism has ever had; indeed, it outbids all the despotisms of the past inasmuch as it expressly aspires to the annihilation of the individual [...] and (drives) the word "justice" into the heads of the half-educated masses like a nail so as to rob them entirely of their reason. [12]

Nietzsche develops an equally clear and frank criticism of the addiction to consumer goods that has arisen in the modern age and of the capitalist mode of production associated with it. All values – finally even humankind itself – are subordinated to the law of supply and demand:

> The man engaged in commerce [...] enquires, in regard to everything that is made, after supply and demand...

> *in order to determine the value of a thing in his own eyes.* This becomes the character of an entire culture [...] It is this of which you men of the coming century will be proud. [13]

The "curse of money", the consumption of commodities and the search for short-lived pleasures combine to create a new "idol", which is worshipped by the entire Western world:

> The West in its entirety has lost the sort of instincts [...] that give rise to a *future*. People live for today, people live very fast -, people live very irresponsibly. And this is precisely what people call "freedom". [14]

But it is, argues Nietzsche, servile and cowardly to worship new gods and idols, as soon as "God is dead", and to seek comfort in those earthly promises of salvation that are nationalism, anti-Semitism, socialism or capitalism. Instead, he urges us to take the radical step of directing rather to ourselves the question of "where we go from here":

> How can we console ourselves, the murderers of all murderers? [...] Do we not ourselves have to become gods [...] ? [15]

Nietzsche's answer to this question is an unequivocal "yes". After the "death of God" we must somehow muster the courage to form and shape our lives solely on our own responsibilities. This means living without allowing our choices to be determined or dictated by those ideologies that have come to take the place of the old gods and idols. In other words, we must draw, in our lives, on our own inner resources alone. What Nietzsche calls "the advent of nihilism" is a challenge that can only be overcome if we step into the place left empty by God. This means raising ourselves up into a new and higher form of being which will no longer be that of Man but rather of what Nietzsche calls "the overman":

Dead are all gods; now we want the overman to live. [16]

The overman is a being who takes full and complete responsibility for himself. But in order to be able to take on this great task of creating one's own sense and meaning, Man as he exists first needs to develop his own capacities and potentialities to the point where such a new personality-type becomes possible. This philosophical conception of an "overman" was so bold and flew so strongly in the face of all that had come before it that it seemed, to many, like madness. It seemed so not just to those who, in Nietzsche's day, still spoke for the Christian churches but even to the most "enlightened" and religiously sceptical of the philosopher's contemporaries. Never before had anyone dared to pose in so emphatic a form the demand that humankind embrace the idea of its developing beyond itself:

> *I teach you the overman*. Human being is something that must be overcome [...] The overman is the meaning of the earth. [17]

Nietzsche urges us to set out upon a dangerous path. On the one hand, we must neither deny nor lose contact with our valuable instincts and our animal origins; but on the other hand, we must look to the future and see to it that we develop further into a new and higher type of human being:

> Mankind is a rope fastened between animal and overman – a rope over an abyss. [18]

Nietzsche himself described himself as someone who "philosophized with a hammer", destroying the old in order to make room for the new. But what is this "new" that lies beyond all ideology and idolworship? How exactly are we to transcend the condition of humanity as we have known it up until now? Nietzsche's answer to this question is impressively clear and succinct:

Become who you are! [19]

Nietzsche does not conceive of this "becoming who one is" in terms merely of one's "finding oneself". Rather, above and beyond this, it is a matter of taking a second, much more important step of unconditionally acknowledging, and committing oneself to developing, one's own potential. For Nietzsche, this means above all that the individual must, no matter how great the resistance encountered, remain resolved to live out the (as he called them) "Dionysically" creative aspects of his own being, his intuitions, and his own noblest and highest goals. It means also that the individual must learn, outside of and above that "herd-animal morality" that has long been synonymous with morality *per se*, to trust once again in his own nature and destiny, which consists in what Nietzsche calls "will to power". Nietzsche sees will to power as a kind of primal force which has pervaded the coming-to-be and passing-away of the world since the very beginning and which is even operative in plants and animals:

> And you yourselves are also this will to power – and nothing besides! [20]

For millennia, the natural unfolding of will to power was hindered and suppressed by Christianity. Now, however – so argues Nietzsche – it is high time that Man accept once again his own true nature. And part of this true nature are the aggressive, conquering, supposedly "evil" aspects of the human character. If we do not acknowledge and affirm also these aspects of ourselves, we are only, as it were, "half-humans". Nietzsche urges on us, then, the "affirmation of life, life whole and not denied or in part" [21]:

> For every strong and natural species of man, love and hate, gratitude and revenge, good nature and anger, affirmative acts and negative acts, belong together. [22]

No one, says Nietzsche, can be "good" all the time. The very act of living is necessarily, to some extent, a living at the cost of others, inasmuch as exploiting a possibility in life is always a kind of seizing of it for oneself. To develop one's own individual possibilities, however, is nothing reprehensible. For this reason, Nietzsche calls for a radical "transvaluation" of everything that has, up until now, passed for moral values – that is to say, a redefinition of "good" and "bad":

What is good? Everything that enhances people's feeling of power, will to power, power itself. What is bad? Everything stemming from weakness. [23]

But where do the limits of this unfettered will to power lie? May the individual go so far as to actually suppress and oppress others? Who or what exactly is this "overman"? Is it really possible to attain in daily life that intensification of lived experience that Nietzsche calls "Dionysian"? And above all: is Nietzsche, in the end, right when he argues that, without our "evil" aspects, we are only half of what a human being might potentially be?

Nietzsche provides impressive answers to all these questions. They are answers which shock and provoke still today.

Nietzsche's Central Idea

The Dionysian Principle and the Apollonian Principle

Nietzsche published his first book, *The Birth of Trag-edy, or Hellenism and Pessimism*, at the age of only twenty-six. Already in this work he discovered the decisive key to his understanding of the world. This key was art – specifically classical Greek tragedy which, he argued, enlightens us as to the true mean-ing of our lives. All human beings, argued Nietzsche, are, like the heroes of these classical Greek tragedies, caught in a livelong struggle between two great prin-ciples, the Apollonian and the Dionysian:

There are two conditions in which art appears in Man like a force of nature [...] as a compulsion to have visions and as a compulsion to an orgiastic state. [24]

For this "compulsion to have visions" stands Apollo, the god of prophecy, of the oracle at Delphi, of planning for the future, and of light; for the "compulsion to an orgiastic state" stands Dionysus, the god of wine and drunken ecstasy. From ancient times Apollo was honoured in Greece as the shining god who presided over Man's forming of his own future: the god of harmony, of the founding of cities, of the sciences, and of cool, organizing Reason. Apollo, says Nietzsche, personifies the principle that gives form and respects limits and measures. Dionysus, on the other hand, as the god of wine and drunken ecstasy, stands for the chaotic creative principle: for overflowing sensuality, for instinct and for uncontrollable passion. Like the typical hero of Greek tragedy, argues Nietzsche, each one of us carries within himself both these principles, which war eternally with one another.

Thus, the hero of classical tragedy aspires to understand, to bring order, and eventually to bring peace to the many vicissitudes and painful struggles of life. Again and again, however, his "Dionysian" side tips this peace and order back into a state of chaotic, orgiastic dance. The tragic hero suffers terribly from this divided state and from the fate it imposes on him because in Ancient Greece – so argues Nietzsche – there was no "higher meaning" to which such a hero could cling and which could explain to him, in logical terms, the vicissitudes and entanglements of his life. For the Greek tragic hero, in other words, there is no "salvation" nor any path leading out of the terrible ups and downs of life. This hero is at the mercy of fate: a fate in which joy and suffering, chaos and control are inextricably involved and entangled with one another.

This image of the hero who constantly struggles but still always founders is the dramatic core of classical Greek tragedy. But how is it that this tragic struggle which forms the core of these ancient theatrical creations still produces such a powerful effect on audiences today? Nietzsche's answer here is very clear:

Take a look! Take a close look! This is your life! This is the hour hand on the clock of your existence! [25]

Classical Greek tragedy, then, reflects our own existence back to us. We struggle, all of us, day by day and yet encounter, again and again, painful setbacks, sicknesses and losses which we bewail without ever being able to ascribe them to some guilty party. The ancient Greeks teach us to accept life in both its positive and its negative aspects and to love it by perceiving it as a kind of "total work of art". Moreover, this tragic beauty, this joyful participation in a life fully inclusive even of life's painful aspects, is something that we experience not just through dramatic tragedy but through music as well:

> The Dionysian, with the primal pleasure it perceives even in pain, is the common womb from which both music and the tragic myth are born. [26]

In classical Greek tragedy, argues Nietzsche, this Dionysian element is embodied by the chorus which expresses, through its song, the aspect of feeling, whereas the action on the stage is, in large measure, an expression of Apollonian order and structure. But with Euripides, Nietzsche goes on, and the specific form of tragic dramaturgy – chorusless and oriented toward reason – that he ushered in, this equilibrium was lost. The feeling for the tragic aspects of life, and indeed the whole Dionysian dimension, was gradually pushed to the sidelines. And with Socrates and Plato there stepped onto the stage of Greek culture what was, in fact, an entirely new type of human being: "the man of theory".

From this point on it was the use of reason that counted as the only path leading upward toward the light of day and toward "the good, the true and the beautiful". The Dionysian desires of the body, by contrast, counted henceforth as dark and as leading "downwards":

Happiness (now) only means: you have to imitate Socrates and establish a permanent state of *daylight* against all dark desires

– the daylight of reason. [...] Any concession to the instincts, to the unconscious, leads *downwards*. [27]

All that is owed to thought and reason now counted as morally good and everything which was done under the impulse of instinct, feeling or intuition became reprehensible. This, argues Nietzsche, was the beginning of a fundamental hostility to the body that was to last many centuries:

The moralism of Greek philosophers from Plato onwards is pathologically conditioned. [28]

Christianity too, following in Platonism's footsteps, demonized all Dionysian impulses as unchaste, as sinful and a cause for guilt. It was only in the mystical music-drama of Wagner – an artist whom Nietsche had long admired and who had, by the time of his writing *The Birth of Tragedy*, become to him a personal friend and a kind of fatherly mentor – that Nietzsche believed he recognized an urgently-needed remembrance of the Dionysian, tragic aspect of Man and a liberating blow against the centuries-long rule of rationalism. It was in honour of Wagnerthat Nietzsche altered, for a time, the title of this his first book to *The Birth of Tragedy Out of the Spirit of Music*. Some years later, however, he quarrelled bitterly with Wagner, when the latter, in Nietzsche's phrase, "collapsed before the cross" in his mystical-Christian opera *Parsifal*, whose hero displays precisely those guilt-feelings and sense of a bad conscience which

Nietzsche considered the Dionysian to represent a break with. With this opera, Nietzsche believed, Wagner had clearly betrayed the spirit of tragedy. Nietzsche felt such fury at this betrayal that he devoted an entire polemical work, *The Case of Wagner*, just to criticizing and condemning his former friend and mentor.

For his own part, Nietzsche held his whole life long to his original contention that the suffering that we experience is not a punishment imposed by God, nor does it imply any personal sin or guilt, but represents merely that tragic quality inherent in life itself which must be accepted for what it is:

Yes, my friends, believe as I do in Dionysian life and in the rebirth of tragedy. The time of Socratic man is past. [...] Now you must only dare to be tragic human beings. [29]

The Emergence of Slave Morality: How Judaism and Christianity Betrayed Life

With their exalting of reason above all else and their repression of Man's Dionysian nature Plato and Socrates represented, in Nietzsche's view, just the beginning of what was to become a truly world-historical "wrong turning". In one of his later works, *On the Genealogy of Morality*, Nietzsche describes how the rise of monotheistic religions, and specifically of Judaic and Christian morality, signified an inexorable alienation of human beings from their own natural way of being and living. Religion, argues Nietzsche, became the gravedigger of the natural human being and his instincts. Already in Plato's philosophy, indeed, we see a suppression of the Dionysian aspect of human life and being; but this philosophy does not yet involve any such notions as a single punishing Godhead, "original sin", or "saints". It is only Judaism and Christianity that turn the tragically heroic human being of the classical era into a human being who is broken, guilty and reduced to utter humility. Whereas, in classical culture, the victorious Achilles was celebrated as "a favourite of the gods", in the Christian culture which succeeded it the models offered for emulation were those of humble, long-suffering individuals who eschewed all violence. Nietzsche sees in this a betrayal of the old aristocratic values:

It was the Jews who, rejecting the aristocratic value-equation (good = noble = powerful = beautiful = happy = blessed), ventured [...] to bring about

a reversal [...] saying; "Only those who suffer are good, only the poor, the powerless, the lowly [...] the suffering, the deprived, the sick, the ugly [...], salvation is for them alone. [30]

Christianity, emerging out of Judaism, damned the development of humankind's natural forces even farther, argues Nietzsche, by demanding of human beings that they live lives pleasing to God; lives of renunciation, modesty and humility. Nietzsche calls this attitude "slave morality" and sets against it the aristocratic "master morality" of the ancient Greeks and Romans, with the latter in particular succeeding, by struggle, resolution and a pitiless attitude both toward themselves and toward other nations, in building an empire that spanned the known world:

So the Romans were the strong and noble, stronger and nobler than anyone who had hitherto lived or been dreamt of on earth. [31]

For this reason, the Romans experienced the new "morality of pity" propagated by the early Christians as something completely unnatural that directly contradicted their own aristocratic attitude. But in the late phase of the Roman Empire, when depraved despots like Nero and Caracalla could no longer provide models for the people, the feeling began to emerge that the powerful were corrupt and power was something reprehensible in itself. The counter-image, then, of a loving God who willingly renounced all power and violence suddenly became very attractive:

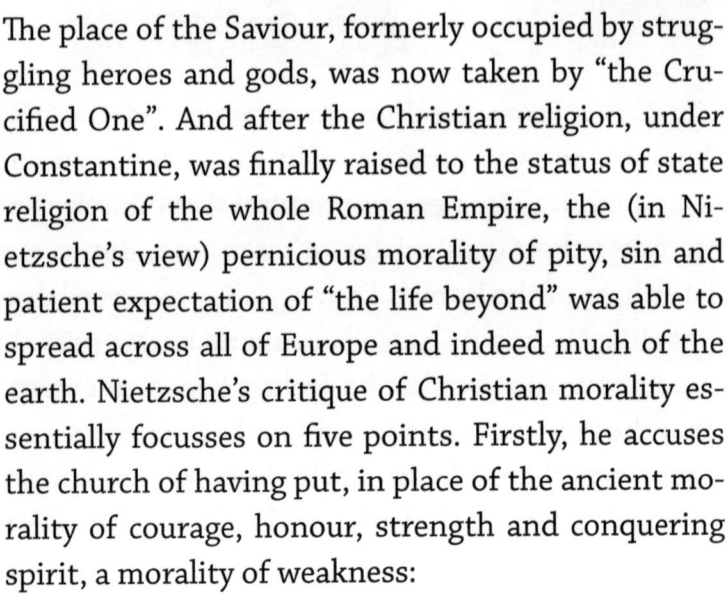

When Nero and Caracalla sat up there the paradox arose: "The lowest man is worth more than that man up there! And the way was prepared for an image of God that was as remote as possible from the image of the most powerful – the god on the cross! [32]

The place of the Saviour, formerly occupied by struggling heroes and gods, was now taken by "the Crucified One". And after the Christian religion, under Constantine, was finally raised to the status of state religion of the whole Roman Empire, the (in Nietzsche's view) pernicious morality of pity, sin and patient expectation of "the life beyond" was able to spread across all of Europe and indeed much of the earth. Nietzsche's critique of Christian morality essentially focusses on five points. Firstly, he accuses the church of having put, in place of the ancient morality of courage, honour, strength and conquering spirit, a morality of weakness:

> I condemn Christianity, I indict the Christian church on the most terrible charges an accuser has ever had in his mouth [...] It has made an un-value out of every value, a lie out of every truth. [33]

Secondly, he reproaches Christianity with having promoted and cultivated pity. But when an individual complies with the commandment to show pity – i.e. when he gives succour to all without acting with the necessary hardness and resolution to root out the causes of the suffering–it normally means just a feeding and a prolongation of the suffering in question:

> Pity a squandering of feeling, a parasite harmful to moral health: "it cannot possibly be our duty to increase the evil in the world". [34]

Pity serves, argues Nietzsche, mostly only to soothe one's own conscience:

> If one does good merely out of pity, it is oneself one really does good to. [35]

The impulse to pity has been deeply implanted in us by the morality of Christianity. Nevertheless, argues Nietzsche, we must recognize it as an "inner weakness" and never yield to it. Insofar, however, as we continue to feel this impulse, inner conflicts necessarily arise, such as that which Nietzsche illustrates by the example of beggars:

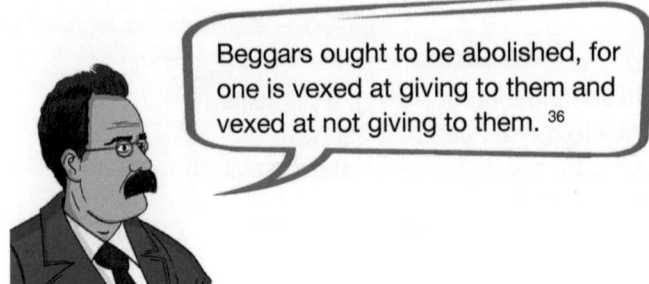

> Beggars ought to be abolished, for one is vexed at giving to them and vexed at not giving to them. [36]

Thirdly, Nietzsche criticizes the Christian church because, with its concepts of guilt, sin and atonement and its demand that people be humble, it has, in Nietzsche's view, ruined the character of human beings. Because, through the constant striving of Christian believers to be "good" and to do what is right in the eyes of God so as to remain unburdened by sin, there has arisen a new type of human being, the *bigot*:

Perhaps there has never before been a more dangerous ideology, a greater mischief *in psychologicis*, than this will to good; one has

reared the most repellent type, the unfree man, the bigot; one has taught that only as a bigot is one on the right path to godhood [...] [37]

Bigotry also manifests itself in the way of thinking characteristic of modern democracies, one concerned with nothing beyond a safe and materially prosperous existence:

> The Christian-democratic way of thinking favours the herd animal [...] It hates all great ventures [...] Thus, it is the most mediocre whose standards of value win out. [38]

Nietzsche's fourth reproach against the Christian church is that, with its promise of eternal life in heaven, it draws all the energy that might have been directed toward the real world "here below" away into the "beyond". Nietzsche sees Jesus as a figure symbolizing "redemption" from nothing less than life itself. In contrast to this "redemption from life" Nietzsche urges us to commit ourselves wholly to life in the "here below", the only true reality. This is tantamount to committing ourselves to that counter-figure to "the Crucified Christ", Dionysus:

> There you have the antithesis [...] The God on the cross is a curse on life, a signpost to seek redemption from life. Dionysus [...] is a *promise* of life. [39]

Fifthly, Nietzsche claims that Christianity – and this is perhaps one of Nietzsche's gravest reproaches – has set in motion, with its ingrained hostility to the body, an ominous process which has had fatal consequences for the human race:

"If thine eye offend thee, pluck it out": [...] the Christian who follows that advice and believes that he has killed his sensuality is deceiving himself; it lives on in an uncanny vampire form and torments him in repulsive disguises. [40]

In giving voice to this suspicion that the feelings, drives and emotions do not simply vanish when they are suppressed for moral reasons but rather "live on in an uncanny vampire form", Nietzsche in fact formulates for the first time an idea which, a few decades later, was to become the whole basis of Freud's psychoanalytic teachings. The life that we have not lived does not merely vanish through our refusing to live it. It can turn against us in dangerous ways. This new view of what Freud was later to call the "psychical economy" of the human mind Nietzsche outlines in the second and perhaps best known of the three essays making up *On the Genealogy of Morality: Guilt, Bad Conscience and Related Matters.*

The Origin of Bad Conscience

For Nietzsche, of course, the conscience cannot be construed as something of divine origin but has rather arisen in the course of evolution from our essentially animal being. Originally, Man was an animal like any other, driven purely by instinct:

Once you were apes, and even now a human being is still more ape than any ape. [41]

But how, then, did there arise what we call a conscience, i.e. that "organ" that can turn itself against our own instincts and thus against our own healthy Dionysian nature? How is such a thing even possible? Of one thing Nietzsche is sure. We are dealing here with a "serious illness":

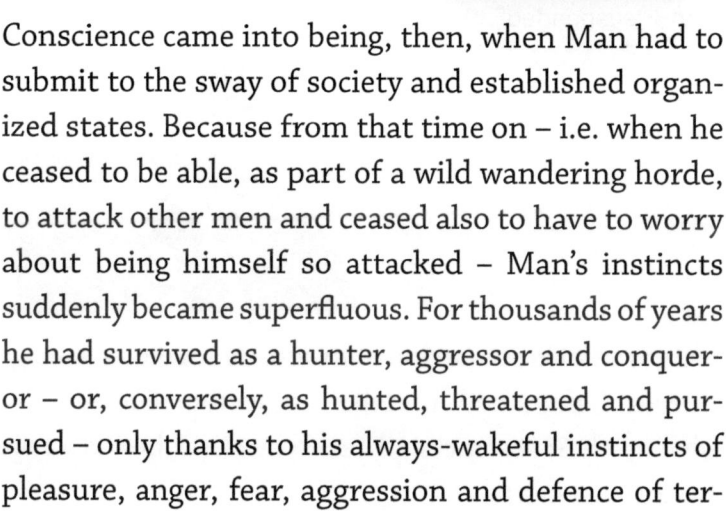

I look on bad conscience as a serious illness to which Man was forced to succumb by the pressure of the most fundamental

of all changes which he experienced – that change whereby he finally found himself imprisoned within the confines of society and peace. [42]

Conscience came into being, then, when Man had to submit to the sway of society and established organized states. Because from that time on – i.e. when he ceased to be able, as part of a wild wandering horde, to attack other men and ceased also to have to worry about being himself so attacked – Man's instincts suddenly became superfluous. For thousands of years he had survived as a hunter, aggressor and conqueror – or, conversely, as hunted, threatened and pursued – only thanks to his always-wakeful instincts of pleasure, anger, fear, aggression and defence of territory. Once organized states had been established, however, he could no longer allow these old reactions and emotions free rein. Nietzsche compares this period of the emergence of human conscience with that distant prehistoric period in which sea animals were forced to migrate to the land and develop new limbs and organs to survive there:

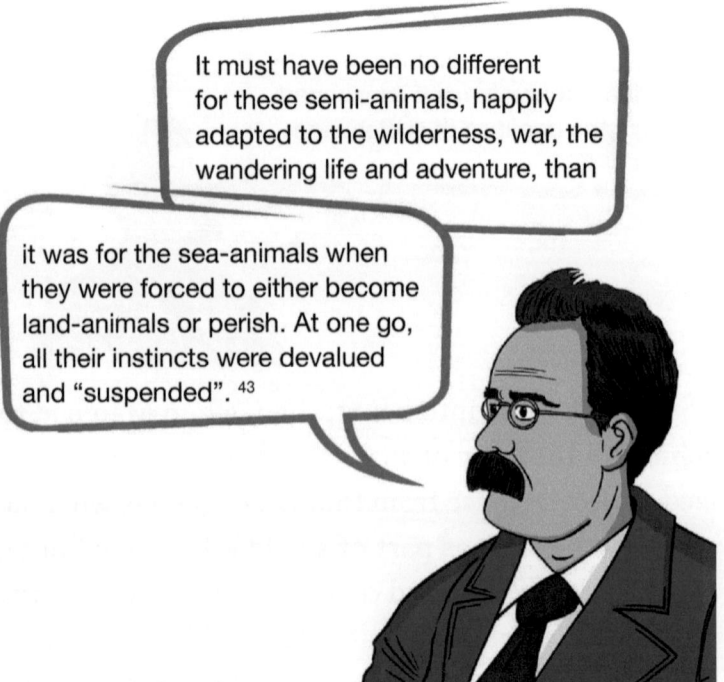

It must have been no different for these semi-animals, happily adapted to the wilderness, war, the wandering life and adventure, than it was for the sea-animals when they were forced to either become land-animals or perish. At one go, all their instincts were devalued and "suspended". [43]

This transitional period – in which formerly savage human beings had, installed in society, suddenly to give up their instincts – Nietzsche describes as a true historical watershed:

I do not think there has ever been such a feeling of misery on earth. [44]

Human beings now found themselves in a world entirely unknown to them. They could no longer fight, individually, with each other nor, as a group, against other groups and had, all of a sudden, lost the guide which had long steered all their actions: "those regulating impulses that unconsciously led them to safety". Out of necessity, then, they formed a new organ:

The poor things were reduced to relying on thinking, inference, calculation and the connecting of cause with effect, that is, to relying on their "consciousness", that most impoverished and error-prone organ! [45]

This "most impoverished organ" is our intellect, our thinking ego or, as the philosophers say, our faculty of reason. Thus, *homo sapiens* was born. In the newly-founded states and societies a man could no longer rob or otherwise despoil his fellow men, no matter how strong an impulse he felt to do it. Even that aggressivity to which Man had owed, for thousands of years, his very survival could no longer be allowed to express itself between citizens of society and was tolerated, at best, in sublimated form in organized sporting events. Instincts became subject to a taboo and their place was taken by reason:

Meanwhile, the old instincts had not suddenly ceased to make their demands. [46]

They still demanded to be expressed and lived out. But what was to be done now with such instincts as inquisitiveness, vigilance, covetousness and aggression?

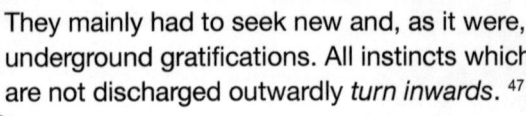

They mainly had to seek new and, as it were, underground gratifications. All instincts which are not discharged outwardly *turn inwards*. [47]

There thus gradually emerged in Man, argues Nietzsche, a whole new dimension of inward experience:

The whole inner world, originally as thin as though stretched between two layers of skin, was expanded and extended itself and

gained depth, breadth and height in proportion to the degree that the external discharge of Man's instincts was *obstructed*. [48]

That the "inner world" was originally "thin as though stretched between two layers of skin" means that primitive Man had almost nothing in the way of "private experiences". He experienced perhaps a certain amazement at the sight of a death, or consternation over a wound when he was bitten by an animal. With the advent of civilization, however, this once-insubstantial "inner life" suddenly, as Nietzsche says, gained depth and breadth and height. All at once, even the tiniest action called forth the question: "is this permitted or forbidden, right or wrong?" Thus, there arose, almost simultaneously with the emergent consciousness of a "self", also a second "inner organ": the so-called "bad conscience":

> Animosity, cruelty, the pleasure in pursuing, raiding, changing and destroying – all this was pitted against the person who had such instincts: *that* is the origin of "bad conscience". [49]

"Bad conscience", then, is nothing divine or metyaphysical but is rather fed by the energy of our own animal drives which we can no longer unleash upon the world around us but must now use to keep our own selves in check, to control our wishes, desires and impulses, and to bring them into harmony with social norms. We do this not willingly but because we know that, otherwise, society will punish us:

> Punishments [...] had the result that all those instincts of the wild, free, roving man were turned backward, *against Man himself*. [50]

The "conscience" then, one might say, was forced into being through the founding of organized states: it is in essence a representative of the state within our own heads, which compels us, through so-called "pangs of conscience", to comply with the rules and the laws. Besides the external structures of punishment, with their policemen, judges and prisons, there exists also a second, inward court of judgment. The work of this latter alone is often enough to ensure that we do not breach the law. Conscience fulfils thereby a very important social function. But we must never forget, argues Nietzsche, what terrible sacrifices this creation of a conscience has involved:

With it [...] the worst and most insidious illness was introduced, one from which mankind has not yet recovered: Man's sickness of Man, of

himself [...] as the result [...] of a declaration of war against all the old instincts on which, up till then, his strength, pleasure and formidableness had been based. [51]

Each human being, Nietzsche argues, today finds himself under the sway of two fateful authorities which govern his instincts and hold them in check: on the one hand, conscience; on the other, reason. Nietzsche has deep reservations regarding both these powers. The human conscience, indeed, cannot be called, in the true sense, a moral authority: it does not create values but only stores up the moral evaluations that it has long since taken over from family, church, school or society:

The conscience [...] merely repeats. It creates no values. [52]

All that is stored away in our conscience in fact comes from outside it:

The content of our conscience is everything that was, during the years of our childhood, regularly

demanded of us, without reason, by people we honoured or feared. It is thus the conscience that excites that feeling of compulsion [...] which does not ask: *why* must I? [53]

The question "why?" is indeed posed by the second of our two "inner authorities": reason. But Nietzsche does not agree with most philosophers that the faculty of reason represents an authority that is just and autonomous. Reason, Nietzsche contends, is a faculty that serves, in the last analysis, only to lie to and fool others or, alternatively, to lie to and fool oneself:

The intellect, as a means of preserving the individual, develops its main powers in dissimulation. [54]

Instead of trusting to our instincts, we accord to the dictates of reason far too great a role in deciding how we act. Reason, we believe, can save us from errors and tricks of the senses because it can perceive the truth through the application of logic. But this belief, insists Nietzsche, is itself an error. The intellect is, in fact, incapable of perceiving anything at all exactly, and certainly not "the truth". It thinks always only in words and propositions. But perhaps – such is Nietzsche's grave suspicion here – words are imprecise by their very nature and equally imprecise, therefore, the "propositions" and "logical truths" of which philosophers have been so proud.

Truth as "Beams and Boards" and Illusion of Language

Every language in the world consists of words and terms. These words and terms we use to name, in one way or the other, the real things around us. But here Nietzsche poses a question of enormous consequence:

Do terms coincide with things? Is language the adequate expression of all realities? [55]

Nietzsche's answer to this question is: no; language is not appropriate to reflect reality. Truth, and all that we consider to be facts, are really just illusions. And these illusions arise from the fact that, since prehistoric times, Man has given, to everything and everyone that he has seen, heard or smelt, a specific name. We designate each thing or person as "this" or "that" and from then on maintain that this name is the "truth" of what is named. We say, for example, that the meadow is green, the world is round, the sun rises, the wolf bites, and maintain that these propositions are true because the designations "green", "round", "rise" and "bite", and likewise the terms "meadow", "earth", "sun" and "wolf", both individually and combined together, reflect reality. But such a "giving of names", Nietzsche argues, is the beginning of a process with fatal consequences:

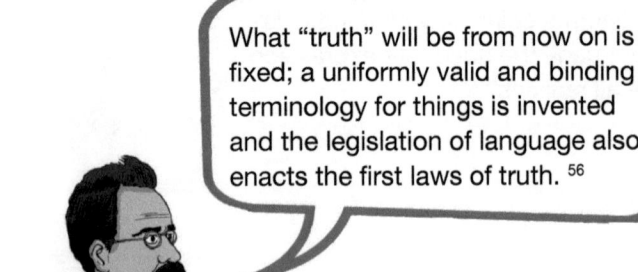

> What "truth" will be from now on is fixed; a uniformly valid and binding terminology for things is invented and the legislation of language also enacts the first laws of truth. [56]

But this constant process of linguistic designation, this violent reduction of everything we encounter to an instance of some "idea" or "concept", is founded, Nietzsche argues, upon a basic error:

> Every concept originates by the equating of the dissimilar. [57]

A concept is just attached to things as if it were a label and the things then treated as if they were identical with the label apposed upon them. But the things to which the label is apposed are in fact very different from one another. Nietzsche illustrates this by the example of the concept "leaf":

> Just as no leaf is ever the same as any other, certainly the concept "leaf" is formed by arbitrarily dropping those individual differences, by forgetting the distinguishing factors, and this gives rise to the idea that, besides

> leaves, there is in Nature such a thing as the "leaf", i.e. an original form according to which all leaves are supposedly woven, sketched, circled off, coloured, painted etc. [...] [58]

The conceptual label "leaf", then, never matches up with the actual reality of the countless individual leaves. Nor is there to be found anywhere in Nature any original leaf which forms all other leaves or somehow lies at the source or basis of these latter. How arbitrary our concepts are can also be seen by the example of how widely these concepts vary between the different languages of the world. In Greenland, for example, there are seven different words corresponding to the English word "snow"; on the other hand, no single word is to be found in French that corresponds to the German word *Gemütlichkeit* :

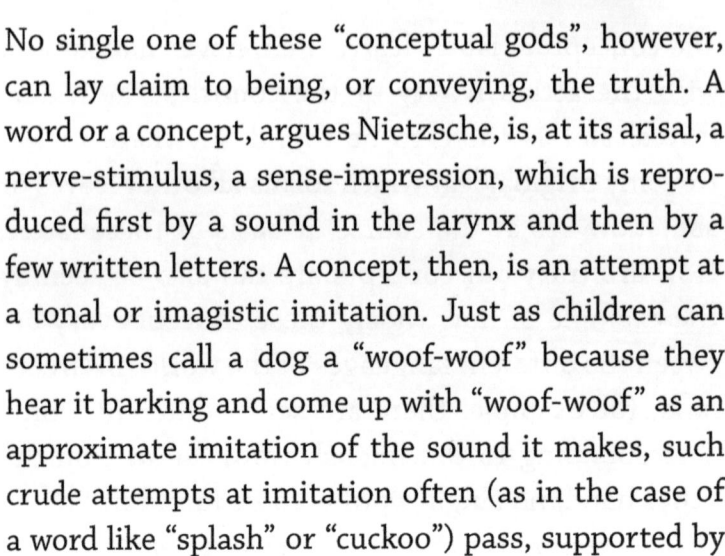

The various languages, juxtaposed, show that words are never concerned with truth, never with adequate expression ; otherwise, there would not be so many languages [...] Thus every nation has (its own) conceptual sky above it and understands by the demand for truth that each conceptual god must be sought only in *his* own sphere. [59]

No single one of these "conceptual gods", however, can lay claim to being, or conveying, the truth. A word or a concept, argues Nietzsche, is, at its arisal, a nerve-stimulus, a sense-impression, which is reproduced first by a sound in the larynx and then by a few written letters. A concept, then, is an attempt at a tonal or imagistic imitation. Just as children can sometimes call a dog a "woof-woof" because they hear it barking and come up with "woof-woof" as an approximate imitation of the sound it makes, such crude attempts at imitation often (as in the case of a word like "splash" or "cuckoo") pass, supported by various other metaphors, into the recognized vocabulary of a language. One might retort to Nietzsche here that no major harm ensues from the fact of such imitations and metaphors' not exactly matching the reality of actual individual dogs or leaves.

Nietzsche would certainly be right, however, to point out in his turn that, however minor the effects, taken singly, of these divergences between abstract term and concrete phenomenon, the cumulative consequences of these divergences can be enormous. Particularly in recent decades, people have begun to talk about how language that was, for centuries, considered as just a convenient system of "labelling" supported, in fact, all along certain structures and practices that were of great consequence for millions of people's lives. It has, for example, been argued that, when the United States Declaration of Independence speaks of "all *men* being created equal", this use of a male term to designate the whole human race has concretely contributed to the disadvantagement of women. As more and more people are aware today, Nietzsche was right in insisting that the words of our languages do not reflect but rather *form*, in terms of certain arbitrary and challengeable metaphors, the worlds that we live in. It is, by the way, this fact that Nietzsche's philosophy is also a critique of reason and language, and of the arbitrary value-systems that reason and language support, that explains why the philosopher of "master morality" – who seems, as a defender of aristocratic values, to naturally belong on the right – is in fact today the philosopher most often cited by forces on the left, such as movements for women's rights and against racial and class discrimination.

The more abstract these metaphors become, Nietzsche goes on to argue, and the more elaborately they are combined in complex verbal propositions, the falser the picture of reality that they give becomes. Nietzsche draws from this a very radical conclusion:

What is truth? A mobile army of metaphors [...] [60]

Even highly intellectual philosophers – indeed, these most of all – produce, in the end, propositions and pronouncements of such extreme abstractness that they can barely be understood, let alone proven or disproven, but which nonetheless give every appearance of being truths. In reality, however, they are only arbitrary language games, in which concepts (which are really only metaphors) are randomly combined with other concepts-cum-metaphors. As if in a game of dice, says Nietzsche, these various concepts/ metaphors are thrown out by the philosophers as supposed reflections of reality, the dots they present added up, and the result given the name reality or truth. But words and propositions, Nietzsche insists, never match reality and can therefore never add up to "the truth". They are and remain only images. Through constant use and re-use, however, these images develop a life of their own:

When the same image has been produced millons of times and has been passed down through many generations of men [...] in the end it has for Man the same significance

as if it were the only necessary image [...] But the hardening and solidification of a metaphor is not at all a guarantee of the necessary and exclusive justification of this metaphor. [61]

Unfortunately, however, Nietzsche goes on, we inevitably forget, in the course of using terms for centuries and millennia, that these terms are indeed not truths but only illusory approximations and metaphors:

Truths are illusions about which it has been forgotten that they *are* illusions. [62]

After Man has blocked out, in the course of time, all awareness that his concepts are only illusions, he then makes a second great mistake. He begins to consider abstract conceptual thought as the only possible access to true reality:

As a "rational" being he now puts his actions under the rule of abstractions. [63]

Descartes' famous proposition "I think, therefore I am" marks the point where mankind fell completely under the sway of abstract thought and of an idolatrous faith in logic. Nietzsche critiques this blind and unconditional faith in language and reason as a cultural wrong turning which leads astray from the real world:

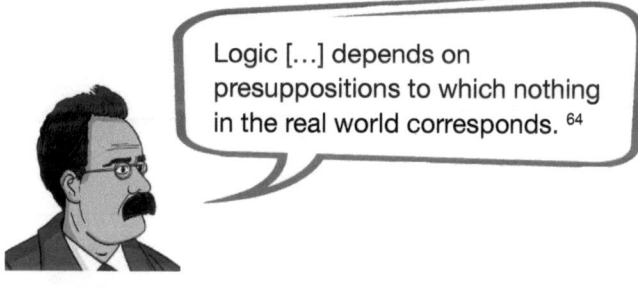

Logic [...] depends on presuppositions to which nothing in the real world corresponds. [64]

Half a century later Wittgenstein, Carnap and other thinkers took up Nietzsche's critique of language and even declared it to be philosophy's most important task. So as to avoid the conceptual errors pointed up by Nietzsche they attempted to establish a new, impeccably exact scientific language which would avoid from the start all false concepts and definitions. The attempt failed.

Nietzsche himself wanted to show, through his critique of language, that linguistically-mediated thought and a faculty of reason operating through logic can lay, in the end, no claim to truth. Instead, he recommends to all free spirits that they seek their bearings rather in the Dionysian spirit, in the chaos of the passions, and in their own intuitions, thus "smashing" the "beam-and-board structure" of conceptuality:

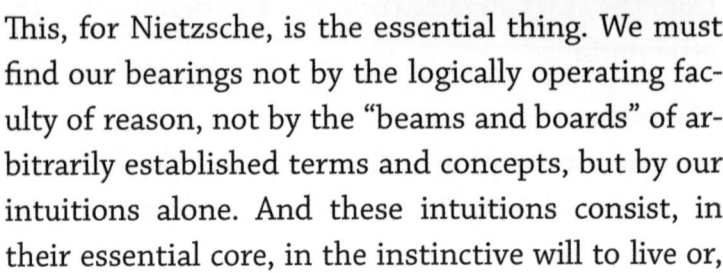

That enormous structure of beams and boards of the concepts to which the poor man clings for dear life is for the liberated intellect just a scaffolding and plaything for his boldest artifices.

And when he smashes it apart, scattering it, and then ironically puts it together again [...] he reveals [...] that he is now guided not by concepts but by intuitions. [65]

This, for Nietzsche, is the essential thing. We must find our bearings not by the logically operating faculty of reason, not by the "beams and boards" of arbitrarily established terms and concepts, but by our intuitions alone. And these intuitions consist, in their essential core, in the instinctive will to live or,

as Nietzsche prefers to define it, the "will to power".
We must admit to ourselves that:

> All "purposes", "aims", "meaning" are only modes of expression and metamorphoses of one will that is inherent in all events: the will to power. [66]

Will to Power as the Essential Feature of All Life

Like Heraclitus, Nietzsche believed that the whole world is an endless process of coming to be and passing away, driven onward by a certain primal force, a certain irrepressible will:

> This world: a monster of energy, without beginning, without end […] is the will to power – and nothing besides! And you yourselves are also this will to power – and nothing besides! [67]

We ourselves, then, are nothing but the will to power. But this will is not just the driving force and capacity of each individual; it is at the same time the fundamental principle underlying reality in all its forms. It is active, Nietzsche contends, equally in animals and plants and even in chemical reactions:

Should we not be permitted to assume this will as a motive cause in chemistry too? [68]

Nietzsche points out even chemicals, when mixed together, display behaviours of discoloration and resistance to discoloration that resemble a struggle for power. The different materials can never leave each other in peace and their struggle always produces some new, third matter. We always observe:

[...] Quanta of force the essence of which consists in exercising power against other quanta of force. [69]

These "quanta of force" – or, alternatively, units of force – are the motive forces behind both micro- and macrocosmos:

I take good care not to talk of chemical "laws". It is rather a question of the establishment of power relations. [70]

Thus, the distances from one another, and the orbital paths, of the various planets can also be calculated from the proportions of their "quanta of force", that is to say, from their respective centrifugal and gravitational attractions. In plants these different "quanta of force" manifest themselves as different energies of growth competing with one another to maximize absorption of the sun's rays. And as an example of will to power in the animal kingdom Nietzsche cites one of the most primitive of all life-forms: the single-cell organism. Not even this earliest and simplest of living beings was peaceful and sufficient unto itself. Also in the protozoon's stretching out of its so-called pseudopodia to surround and absorb some source of nourishment Nietzsche recognizes the will to power:

> Appropriation and assimilation are above all a desire to overwhelm, a forming, shaping, and reshaping, until at length that which has been overwhelmed has entirely gone over into the power domain of the aggressor and has increased this latter. [71]

Nietzsche sees this same fundamental principle of all life manifesting itself in the tree stretching its branches toward the sky, the amoeba absorbing nourishment with its pseudopodia, the buffalo grazing in the meadow, or the wolf killing a doe:

> Life, as the form of being most familiar to us, is specifically a will to the accumulation of force. [72]

> All events that result from intention are reducible to *the intention to increase power.* [73]

This applies, of course, also – indeed, above all – to human beings. Nietzsche lays particular emphasis on the fact that accumulation of force here means not just self-preservation but, above and beyond this, the securing, intensifying and improving of a state of life:

> Physiologists should think again before positing "the instinct of self-preservation" as the cardinal drive in an organic creature. A living thing wants above all to *discharge* its force. [74]

And this discharging of force and applying of it to reality is never selfless but always impinges upon one's environment and specifically upon one's fellow human beings:

One furthers one's ego always at the expense of others. [75]

Daily life often admits of no other possibility. To be a human being at all, argues Nietzsche, means inevitably to take possession of others, to touch them, to help or hinder them, to guide, enthuse or offend them. To imagine that one could live one's whole life unsullied by any wrong done to others is, he says, to delude oneself:

Life always lives at the expense of other life – he who does not grasp this has not taken even the first step toward honesty with himself. [76]

The person, for example, who applies for a position as head of his department and is successful cannot help but cause bitter disappointment in the other applicants. To marry a beautiful woman with whom, perhaps, someone else is in love is happiness, indeed, for oneself but by that same token profound unhappiness for the unsuccessful suitor. And if one happens to find – as is, sadly, often enough the case – that one loves, perhaps without wanting to or even being aware of it, one of one's own children more than another, the less loved will suffer from this his or her whole life long. These few examples suffice to show that it is impossible to live without doing some harm to others. Even an Olympic athlete bound to abide by the principles of fairness will enjoy his or her fairly-won victory partly because this victory overshadows the unvictorious competitors. Will to power, then, understood as the necessary furtherance of life and the self, is nothing wicked and must not be morally condemned:

The free human being accepts and embraces their own will to power and their own unfolding of all their forces:

> A free human being is a *warrior* – How is freedom measured in individuals and in peoples? It is measured by the resistance that needs to be overcome, by the effort that it costs to stay *on top*. [78]

Among the examples that Nietzsche cites of peoples and nations who have unfolded and developed, in the face of great resistance, their own will to power are ancient Rome, Venice and the city-states of Northern Italy:

> Those great hothouses for the strong, for the strongest type of people ever to exist, aristocratic communities in the style of Rome and Venice, understood

> freedom in precisely the sense I understand the word: as something that you have and do *not* have, that you *will*, that you *win* [...]. [79]

This winning for oneself of what one wills but does not yet have applies, for Nietzsche, not just to physical territory but also, and above all, to intellectual and spiritual new frontiers. Thus, Nietzsche considers the era of the Renaissance in the flourishing city-states of Northern Italy to be a prime historical instance of the self-unfolding of human will to power:

Today's European is still worth considerably less than the Renaissance European. [80]

Never in any era since the Renaissance, argues Nietzsche, have such great and passionate efforts been made to overcome all limits and boundaries in so many spheres of science, art, culture, literature and architecture:

The Italian Renaissance contained within it [...] liberation of thought, disrespect for authorities, victory of education over the arrogance of ancestry, enthusiasm for science [...], unfettering of the individual (and) a passion for truthfulness [...] [81]

Leonardo da Vinci, Botticelli, Michelangelo, Brunelleschi and many others worked tirelessly to raise Renaissance Man to ever greater heights. The unfolding of human power, then, is something that can occur as much in the artistic sphere as it can in the political:

I assess a man by the quantum of power and abundance of his will [...] I assess the power of a will by how much resistance, pain, torture it endures and knows how to turn to its advantage. [82]

But what are the proper limits to this "will to power"? May I go so far as even to kill others to achieve my ends? There can indeed be situations, Nietzsche argues, in which the achievement of some noble goal is more important than my own or others' personal survival. Thus, Nietzsche describes as "the basic instinct of all strong natures" the sense that:

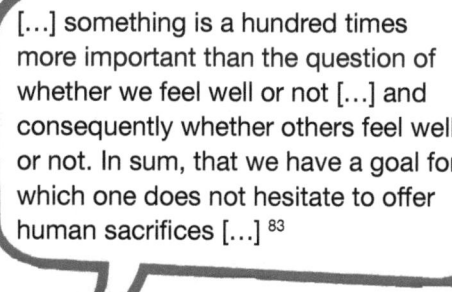

[...] something is a hundred times more important than the question of whether we feel well or not [...] and consequently whether others feel well or not. In sum, that we have a goal for which one does not hesitate to offer human sacrifices [...] [83]

It sounds, at first, brutal when Nietzsche urges us to live out our will to power and not to hesitate, should it prove necessary, to offer human sacrifices to achieve our goal. But there are, in fact, situations in which this is required. The test case in this regard for Nietzsche's own nation, Germany, was not so much, as it might at first appear to be, the period of Hitler's dictatorship as the period of left-wing terrorism – the so-called "years of lead" – that followed it forty years later. The German Chancellor of this period, Helmut Schmidt, was placed in just such a situation by the major German terrorist group of the day, the "Red Army Faction" whose activity reached a crescendo in the so-called "German Autumn" of 1977. With the main leaders of the "Faction" already in jail, the remaining members of the group carried out more and more violent operations to pressure the government into releasing the prisoners: in September the armed abduction of leading industrialist Hanns Martin Schleyer, and in October, through the proxy of an allied Arab group, the hijacking of an airplane carrying eighty-six passengers. As Schmidt himself later testified, these actions placed him in a position much like that of the Nietzschean individual after the death of God and the end of the firm moral orientation God had provided. "Whether one should pay for the lives of innocent people in an aeroplane," he told a writer for the German magazine *Die Zeit* in 2007, "the price of letting criminals go free who might then go on to commit other crimes – this is a question one finds no answer to either in the Constitution or in such holy books as the Bible, the Koran or the Thora." [84]

Schmidt took on the great moral responsibility of refusing to negotiate with either group of terrorists. In the latter case, the skill of German counter-terrorist forces who stormed the plane and rescued all the hostages allowed his decision to emerge as unequivocally the right one. In the former, however, the moral dilemma was brought home with terrible force. Faced with Schmidt's refusal to be blackmailed, the "Red Army Faction" went ahead and murdered Schleyer. The Chancellor had to live with his share of responsibility in this death for the rest of his life. As Nietzsche had urged, he had acted in the service of a higher purpose without regard to the lives of other. Schmidt made it clear, however, that he would set, in such a situation, no higher price on his own life or those of his loved ones. In the same interview, he revealed that, during his chancellorship, the standing order had been given to all state authorities that "if Herr Schmidt or his wife are ever abducted, no exchange or deal for their lives is to occur". [85]

In certain extreme situations, then, will to power can require that we sacrifice others – and indeed ourselves – in the service of some higher goal. Thus far, it is hard to disagree with Nietzsche. But there are also passages in Nietzsche's work which go much farther than this and in which the act of killing no longer serves any concrete higher goal. Often, we find Nietzsche praising the murder of other human beings in war as a good means for "training the character" and of restoring energy and vigour to peoples that have become dull and soft through the habits of civilized life. To this end, he even describes war as "indispensable":

War indispensable – [...] For the present we know of no other means by which that rude energy that characterizes the military camp [...] that murderous cold-bloodedness with a good conscience [...]

that proud indifference to great losses, to one's own existence and that of one's friends [...] could be communicated more surely or strongly than every great war communicates these things. [86]

In passages like these Nietzsche portrays war as an antidote to decadence. Without stating explicitly whether entering into a war is a morally defensible move or not, he points out nonetheless that war helps nations to acquire "that rude energy that characterizes the military camp" and a "murderous cold-bloodedness with a good conscience". Disturbing as these statements of Nietzsche's may be, the passage in which he makes them also contains a prognosis about the future of Europe which, in the decades after his death, proved astonishingly accurate:

[…] (It will increasingly be revealed) that so highly cultivated and, for that reason, necessarily feeble humanity as that of the present-day European requires

not merely war but the greatest and most terrible wars – thus, a temporary relapse into barbarism – if the means to culture are not to deprive them of their culture and of their existence itself. [87]

A passage like this one from the year 1878 – in which Nietzsche predicts for Europe "the greatest and most terrible wars" and a "relapse into barbarism" and even goes so far as to legitimate these terrible things as tonics restoring strength to European culture – surely merits its description as "the dark side" of this great philosopher. Some years later, in *On the Genealogy of Morality* from 1887, an even darker side is revealed. In this late work he evokes in grotesquely enthusiastic terms the depredations of various ancient warrior castes living out without inhibition their will to power and inner nature as "beasts of prey":

At the centre of all these noble races we cannot fail to see the beast of prey, the magnificent *blond beast* avidly prowling round for spoil and

victory. This hidden centre needs release from time to time. The beast must out again, must return to the wild. Roman, Arabian, Germanic, Japanese nobility – in this requirement they are all alike. [88]

It is undeniable that these passages in which Nietzsche expresses such sentiments with regard to the Samurai of old Japan, the Vikings of Scandinavia, the martial elites of ancient Rome and Germany, and the warrior-kings of the Homeric epics were, at the very least, grist to the mill of his philosophy's appropriation, some decades after his death, by Mussolini's fascists, Hitler's National Socialists and other movements and nations practicing and glorifying war. Nietzsche's later work, in fact, is full of such problematical passages, such as *Thus Spoke Zarathustra's* provocative turning on its head of the Christian doctrine that the weak and suffering must be suc-coured and raised up:

But I say: if something is falling, one should give it a push! [89]

Particularly in recent years this "dark side" of Ni-etzsche has tended to be underplayed in the com-mentaries and analyses devoted to his work. There has been, indeed, an enormous movement during the last forty years to distinguish and disentangle a "real Nietzsche" from the Nietzsche who had been, in the early and middle years of the 20th Century, so enthusiastically taken up by fascism. The "aris-tocratic values" propounded by Nietzsche – so runs the main interpretative line adopted by this "new Nietzscheanism" – consist essentially in an "aristoc-racy of the soul" and have little or nothing to do with physical force or martial domination. In the light of the passages which we have just cited, however, it is clear that this interpretation of Nietzsche is quite as false, in the end, as is the interpretation of his thought as a mere manifesto for fascism.

Given the many different moods and perspectives that went to make up Nietzsche's aphoristic, anti-systematic philosophical writing, it was inevitable that this latter came to include a large number of very provocative passages. Nietzsche's thought is like a mine in which there are to be found not just seams of gold and silver but also deposits of baser matter such as coal or granite and many a dangerous and even poisonous substance besides. Each interpreter of Nietzsche tends to "mine" this thought only for whatever fits his or her own interpretation. One must, however, try to see Nietzsche whole. And this means that one should not try to "hush up" his occasional flirtations with the glorification of war, conquest, predation and all the evil side of history and human nature, even if one must also be careful not to ascribe to them too central a place in his thought. Nietzsche's writings leave us in no doubt that this great philosopher's mentality or character was such that war possessed a certain sentimental appeal for him. But this does not suffice to make him a Fascist or a Nazi.

Because Nietzsche's writings leave us in no doubt either that he condemned more firmly than did any other writer of his day the "bovine nationalism" which was on the rise at his time of writing or, as he says, the "national dementia" which had it in itself to destroy the very idea of Europe. He was particularly irked by how Prussia's military victory over France in 1870, which gave Bismarck the impetus he'd been seeking to found a German Empire, had ushered in an era of "Teutonic" grandiosity and self-importance. Indeed, Nietzsche was of the view that, if any European nation had a right to be patriotic, then it was the defeated party, France, in this war of 1870 in which he had himself participated as a medical orderly. Nietzsche had great esteem and reverence for French culture. His attitude on the issue of nationalism and internationalism, then, was clear. He saw himself and those who accepted his ideas not as "lovers of humanity", but decidedly not as nationalists or racists either:

[...] We should never dare to allow ourselves to speak of our "love of humanity" [...] But on the other hand we

are not nearly "German" enough [...] to advocate nationalism and racial hatred [...] In a word – and let this be our word of honour – we are *good Europeans* [...] [90]

But the clearest position that Nietzsche takes against every fascist or nationalist ideology is that implicit in his theory of *ressentiment*. Will to power is the most basic instinct driving every human being. But whereas strong and free spirits unfold and develop their power creatively and live out their own values, the weak and the unfree repress all their instinctual drives toward power and cling slavishly to the "herd morality" that their society prescribes to them. At a certain point, however, when the pressure of this conformity becomes too great, this weak and unfree "herd" develops feelings which Nietzsche, borrowing a term from the French tradition of philosophical psychology which he held in such high esteem, describes as feelings of *ressentiment*. These are feelings of envy and hatred to which the weak and the unfree can give free rein wherever they bond together into a fanatical mass:

[...] Fanaticism is the only "strength of the will" that even the weak and insecure can be brought to attain [...] [91]

The weak, in other words – or, as Nietzsche also sometimes refers to them, "underprivileged" – concentrate all the dammed-up energies of the lives they have been too weak to live and direct them resentfully against others: against other nations, against "free spirits", against Jews, and indeed against anyone who can serve as a surface on which to project their own discontent. By degrading others, they attempt to "raise themselves for a moment above their own wretchedness" and "produce in themselves a feeling of [...] importance":

There are proud fellows who, to produce in themselves a feeling of dignity and importance, always require others whom they can dominate and rape [...] in order to raise themselves for a moment above

their own wretchedness. To this end, one person has need of a dog, a second of a friend, a third of a wife, a fourth of a party, and a very rare type of a whole era. [92]

In short, then: will to power is the basic force underlying all that lives. It is active throughout the cosmos:
in plants, animals and human beings. For human beings, everything depends upon not suppressing this
will to power or dissipating it in mean-minded acts
of *ressentiment* but rather allowing it to develop in all
its creative force and realizing its highest potential.
Because just this is the path that leads to a higher
type of human being, whom Nietzsche calls "the
Overman".

The Overman –
Facets of a New Art of Living

Who is this Overman? What is it that sets him apart?
Nietzsche's answer to this question is multi-layered
and highly poetic. It is above all in what is perhaps
his central work, *Thus Spoke Zarathustra*, that he ex-
pounds his vision of the Overman. At the beginning
of this work, we see its protagonist, the prophet Zarathustra, descend, after ten years' silence, from the
mountains amidst the people of the cities and pro-
claim to these people the onset of a new Dionysian

age. A "higher being", he tells them – the Overman – should and must, in future, replace mere Man and take over from this latter.

Because modern Man, once he has recognized that "God is dead" and that he can no longer find his salvation in the old religious values, has just three possibilities. The first is: he finds the bearings that religion can no longer offer him in such "substitute religions" and "false gods" as nationalism, anti-Semitism, socialism, social Darwinism or the petty-bourgeois values of the consumer society. The second is: he succumbs to nihilism; his life stagnates; he becomes apathetic, purposeless and resigned to this lack of feeling and purpose. But there is a third possibility, and this is the one that Nietzsche urges upon us. It is the daring gamble of an entirely new orientation. We must take a great step forward: the step toward the Overman. The place both of God and of the new "false gods" must be taken by this latter, who discovers and unchains his own creative capacities:

Dead are all gods. Now we want the Overman to live. [93]

As soon as we human beings realize that with the "death of God" all earlier systems of values have also died and that nothing and no one any longer can tell us how we should live, we have no choice but to begin to trust in ourselves alone. The moment of this realization is the moment in which the Overman is born. The Overman, then, is at the same time both "the victor over God and the victor over nothingness". He establishes his own law, decides the course of the future, gives birth to new values:

Whoever reflects upon the way in which the type Man can be raised to his greatest splendour and power will grasp first of all that he must place himself outside of morality [...] [94]

Nietzsche's Overman, then, acts in total independence and wagers everything upon the attempt to make his own impulses bear fruit in his real existence. This means that he often leaves the "comfort zone" of the society around him:

[...] The secret for harvesting from existence the greatest fruitfulness and the greatest enjoyment is – to *live dangerously*! [95]

But even if the Overman as Nietzsche conceives of him "lives dangerously" and according to his own choice and judgment, he is not to be confused – a confusion that 20th-Century English translations of Nietzsche's books encouraged for many years by rendering Nietzsche's term as "Superman" – with the heroic "Man of Steel" well-known from films and comic books. Nietzsche's Overman is neither a circus strongman nor a hero admired and honoured by all. On the contrary, the Overman as Nietzsche portrays him is rather an outsider, even an outlaw: a tragic figure tested by pain and suffering. Nor does he come, like the comic-book hero, from some distant star far removed from normal earthly existence. In fact, there are just five characteristics that distinguish the Overman from a normal, everyday human being. Firstly, happiness is not his priority in life. Secondly, the laws he obeys are laws he gives to himself. Thirdly, he struggles passionately for his highest values and is prepared to make great sacrifices for them. Fourthly, he has no vanity and cares nothing for others' opinion of him. And fifthly, he loves life.

In the last analysis, perhaps the only thing that Nietzsche's Overman has in common with the comic-book hero Superman is a certain strength of mind:

It is richness in personality, abundance in oneself, overflowing and bestowing, instinctive good health and affirmation of oneself that produce great sacrifice and great love [...] [96]

The strength that distinguishes the Overman, then, is no physical but above all a mental and spiritual strength. Since he is committed to the unfolding of will to power, he tries to develop his own highest potential against resistances both inside and outside of himself. Nietzsche states, indeed, writing of this will to power, that

The weaker is persuaded by its own will to serve the stronger [...] [97]

But with these terms "weaker" and "stronger" – along with other related terms such as "master and slave morality" and indeed "Overman" itself – Nietzsche does not intend to evoke any group, nation or race but rather individual strong personalities who resolutely take their stand against "the morality of the herd", against the "leader principle", and against the materialism of consumer society. What is more, the "stronger" easily become themselves the "weaker" when they are forced to live as outsiders confronted by all the terrible power of a society where the "majority" and the "herd animal" rules:

> The strongest [...] are weak when opposed by (the) organized herd instincts (of) [...] the weak, by the vast majority. [98]

By "weakness", then, Nietzsche means, in the last analysis, *ressentiment*, slave morality, the hate and envy that are directed toward others as a means of "raising oneself above wretchedness". The Overman, by contrast, is distinguished by the fact that he achieves a radical self-liberation from those "herd moralities", represented by both Christianity and modern mass society, which have stood, for centuries, in the way of the development of higher beings like himself:

Christianity [...] has waged a *war to the death* against this *higher* type of person; it has banned all the basic instincts of this type [...] [99]

But it is with just these "basic instincts" – animalistically Dionysian as they are – that Man needs to reconnect if he is really to develop his creative powers. Nietzsche's "overman", then, is, on the one hand, an aristocrat, a master, an immoralist, a bold discoverer and conqueror but, on the other hand, a creative, Dionysian, intuitive, artistic individual, brimming over with love. In short, considered objectively, he displays certain sharply mutually contradictory aspects – and these contradictions are not, in every case, pacified and brought into harmony with one another. This becomes clear from the words that Nietzsche places in the mouth of his Zarathustra:

The overman is in my heart, *that* is my first and my only concern – and *not* human beings, not the neighbour, not the poorest, not the most suffering, not the best. [100]

The overman, then, whom Nietzsche proclaims here through the mouth of Zarathustra is not that poor and suffering "fellow man" who forms the object of pity and brotherly love; nor, however – and this is the surprising turn taken by this passage from Nietzsche's central philosophical statement – is he "the best" of men. For whether this "best of men" is construed as the most respected, the richest, the most handsome or the most influential, in none of these cases does he coincide with the passionately Dionysian overman, who suffers ardently for his life's work, and for this life's work alone:

[...] The "higher nature" of the great man lies in being different, in incommunicability

[…] not in an effect of any kind – even if he made the whole globe tremble. [101]

"Incommunicability" – that is to say, standing for a higher purpose the nature of which one can, perhaps, no longer fully get across to others – is what defines and constitutes the overman, not the effects he achieves. Dictators, then, who may indeed "make the whole globe tremble", are not thereby overmen in Nietzsche's sense, any more than are great capitalist tycoons:

Just look at these superfluous! They acquire riches and yet they become poorer! […] These impotent, impoverished ones! [102]

What is heroic in the overman consists, in the end, in the fact that he places all the strength of his will in the service of his highest goal. It does not matter at all, then, what privations he has to suffer or whether or not he achieves happiness:

People don't strive for happiness. Only the English do. [103]

With this remark, Nietzsche is taking a sideswipe at Utilitarianism, a characteristically British school of philosophy which remains influential still today. Utilitarianism claims that each action should be judged by the extent to which it serves the "utility", and thereby the happiness, of the greatest number of people. For Nietzsche, this is "morality for those with the souls of shopkeepers". In direct contrast to this, the Dionysian individual throws himself passionately into the service of the cause he has chosen without the least regard for his utility or his happiness. He reckons neither with praise nor recognition:

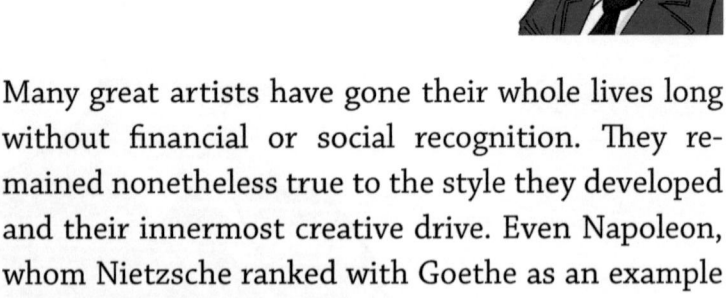

Passionate people think little of what others are thinking. The condition they are in raises them above vanity. [104]

Many great artists have gone their whole lives long without financial or social recognition. They remained nonetheless true to the style they developed and their innermost creative drive. Even Napoleon, whom Nietzsche ranked with Goethe as an example of a truly great man, failed in the end and was banished to Saint Helena.

To live out one's will to power, then, and to develop, in Dionysian manner, all one's inner potential does not mean that one will be able to assert oneself triumphantly against the world. Indeed, generally speaking, neither social success or political power or personal wealth are important concerns for the overman. His concern is rather with a quite new type of intensification of individual existence. He aspires to give, as an individual, everything that he has to give: to passionately express outwardly all that he is inwardly. It matters little to him, in the end, that, in doing this, he often remains misunderstood or even fails spectacularly. He loves even the resistances that he encounters in life, on which he can wear away his energies – loves perhaps, precisely these above all else. In short, he loves life's suffering to the same degree as he loves its joy:

> My formula for human greatness is *amor fati* [...] Not just to tolerate necessity [...] but to love it. [105]

The Eternal Recurrence

The phrase *amor fati* means "love of one's destiny". And this is what is essentially at issue also in Nietzsche's much-discussed theory of "the eternal recurrence". The point of this doctrine is that we need to accept and embrace life even where it is seen to harbour no "higher meaning" beyond itself. Nietzsche rejected this notion of a "higher meaning" behind or beyond life not only in the form of the notion of a God creating and guiding Nature but also in the more modern form of the notion that the course of evolution is leading the human race upward toward some fixed goal:

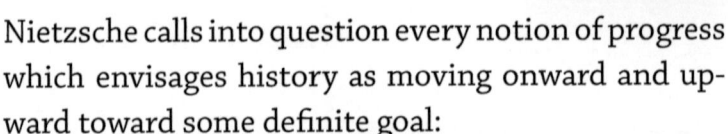

> Humanity does *not* represent a development for the better, does not represent something stronger or higher the way people these days think it does. "Progress" is just a modern idea, which is to say a false idea. [106]

Nietzsche calls into question every notion of progress which envisages history as moving onward and upward toward some definite goal:

> We deny end-goals. If existence had one, it would have to have been reached. [107]

If history,Nietzsche is arguing here, had, for example, the end-goal of the creation of an ideal society, this end-goal would surely have long since been attained. Indeed, for Nietzsche even the overman is not to be conceived of as the result of an upward movement tending toward some goal but only as "a stroke of luck":

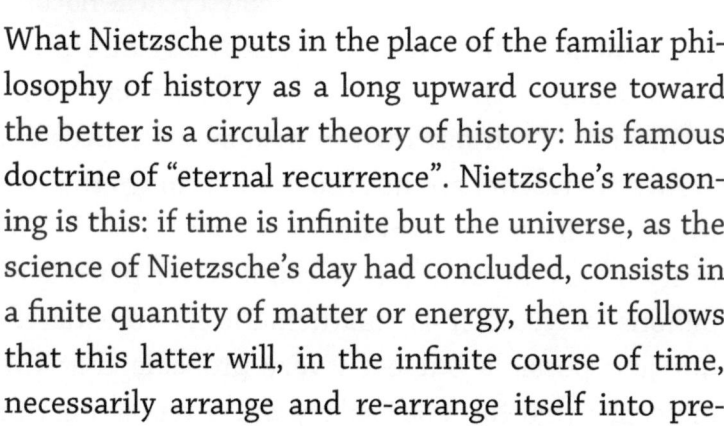

> There is a continuous series of individual successes in the most varied places on earth [...] (in which) a *higher type* does in fact present itself:
>
> a type of overman in relation to humanity in general. Successes like this, real strokes of luck, were always possible and perhaps will always be possible. [108]

What Nietzsche puts in the place of the familiar philosophy of history as a long upward course toward the better is a circular theory of history: his famous doctrine of "eternal recurrence". Nietzsche's reasoning is this: if time is infinite but the universe, as the science of Nietzsche's day had concluded, consists in a finite quantity of matter or energy, then it follows that this latter will, in the infinite course of time, necessarily arrange and re-arrange itself into precisely the same patterns and configurations over and over again, forever.

The weather, for example, consists in a very limited number of orderings and re-orderings of matter through various chemical and physical processes. And it is by no means rare that one's reaction to the weather forecast is one of "déjà vu" ("not this again!") But even if one stretch of poor weather may be only roughly, and not precisely, identical to another stretch of such weather a few weeks before, it is at least highly probable that, over hundreds or thousands of years, an absolutely exact repetition of meteorological conditions might really occur. Even beautiful sunsets may not be so unique as we like to think they are. Photographs reveal something very like an eternal recurrence of the same thing.

But it is not only such recognizedly cyclical natural phenomena as the weather, sunrises and sunsets and the seasons of the year that exemplify this eternal recurrence. Even our own individual existences (so argues Nietzsche) are not the unique things that we would gladly have them be, once one takes the infinity of cosmic time into account. Over periods of billions of years it is, mathematically considered, not just possible but even very probable that the molecules that form our galaxy will, after having run through all the other potential combinations, form themselves once again into a combination which reproduces, down to the tiniest detail, the combination in which they exist at the present moment:

> Our world consists in the *ashes* of countless living beings; thus, even though the animate world is so small a sphere compared to the whole, *everything* has at one or another time been animate, and so it goes on. [...] [109]

> Existence, just as it is, without meaning or goal, but inevitably recurring over and over again, without ever finding its *finale* in nothingness: "the eternal recurrence of the same". [110]

These lines are (as is so often the case with Nietzsche) provocative and difficult to digest. Firstly, he says that our existence is recurrent and thus not

at all unique. Secondly, he states that it is an existence played out in a world without meaning or purpose. Nor, he adds, is there any sort of "*finale*", not
even the "*finale* of nothingness", in which a sense for
existence is after all revealed or the senseless eternal
recurrence at least finally comes to an end.

Despite all this, however, Nietzsche urges us not to
lapse, in the face of the absurdity of these recurring
cycles, into an attitude of passive resignation but
rather to affirm this tremendous process, to let the
feeling of being part of it suffuse us, and even to find
joy in this feeling. Nietzsche describes, in his characteristically poetic language, the eternal recurrence as
something which binds us together with Nature, the
cosmos and the entire universe, as something

[…] set in a definite space as a definite force, and not a space that might be "empty" here or there, but rather as force throughout, as a play of forces and waves of forces, at the same time one and many, increasing here and at the same time decreasing there, a sea of forces flowing and rushing together, eternally changing, eternally flooding back, with tremendous years of recurrence [...] [111]

Astonishingly, this doctrine is not in contradiction with Darwin's theory of evolution. For Nietzsche as for Darwin the world is in constant transformation. But Nietzsche thinks in larger, in positively gigantic, spans of time. If for example, as science foresees, our sun will one day become cold and dead and the earth that orbits it along with it, then there will begin at the same time, in millions of other solar systems, new processes of evolution, some of which will be exact repetitions of earlier processes. In the great crescendo of one of the longest passages found in the notes of his final years Nietzsche describes this eternal recurrence as just another way of conceiving of that fundamental force that he also calls "will to power":

> This, my *Dionysian* world of the eternally self-creating, the eternally self-destroying [...], without goal [...], do you want a *name* for this world? [...] *This world is will to power – and nothing besides*! And you yourselves are also this will to power – and nothing besides! [112]

The doctrine of eternal recurrence has, moreover, a significance – and a very valuable one – for the way in which each of us, personally, lives his or her life. Nietzsche rejects, indeed, the ideas of reincarnation and life after death. But we can still pose to ourselves the existential question of whether we really wish our own individual existence, just as it is in every detail, to recur again and again throughout eternity.

Of What Use Is Nietzsche's Discovery for Us Today?

Is Nietzsche Right? – Is Humanity Not Complete Without "Evil"?

Nietzsche's philosophy is like a mountain torrent which seems at first to sweep away all values and to leave no stone of our moral systems standing. Nothing is sacred to him. But where, in the end, does Nietzsche's "transvaluation of all values" take us? Is, in the end, absolutely everything permitted: even such evil as robbery and murder? Nietzsche answers this question with a counter-question:

> "Thou shalt not rob! Thou shalt not kill!" – Such words were once held holy [...] But I ask you [...] is there not in all life itself – robbing and killing? [113]

It is certainly true that robbery and murder have been part of human life since the dawn of Man and that no end to this situation is in sight. Crime statistics in the USA, for example, record over fifteen thousand murders every year. But do not – it might be argued – these fifteen thousand murders among a population of over three hundred million represent just exceptions proving the rule that people, generally, live non-violently? Were this argument accepted, then it would follow that "evil" does not, as Nietzsche suggests it does, form an essential part of Man and of Man's culture. Man in his civilized state – such is the account of things taught already in our schools – tends to organize his life on cooperative, dialogical, non-violent principles. Corporal punishment, for example, has now passed almost entirely out of use both in educational and in penal institutions.

All this seems to give reason for hope. But when one turns on the television in the evening, one gets another picture entirely. It is not just on the early evening news that one is presented with images of violent crimes, terrorist attacks and wars. The "entertaining" part of an evening's TV programming is, one discovers, packed even more tightly with such images. Anyone "zapping" through the various TV channels will be treated to an impressive gallery of "evil": a constant stream of shouts, threats, blackmail, robbery, kidnapping, beatings, shootings, rapes and even cannibalism. Secret agents, bank robbers, serial killers, zombies, mutants, killer sharks and aliens all go about their dastardly work. But why is this? What is it about the criminal, the aggressive and the evil which fascinates us so much that TV stations, night after night, deliver this and very nearly only this into our living rooms? Could Nietzsche be right after all? Is evil an essential part of our nature?

> For human beings are the cruellest animals. Tragic plays, bullfights and crucifixions have always made them feel best on earth. [114]

In the Middle Ages, indeed, no spectacle drew a larger audience than a beheading or a drawing and quartering and in ancient Rome bloody gladiatorial contests and throwings to the lions attracted thousands. Today, the place of these cruel spectacles is taken, perhaps, by heavyweight boxing matches or by TV cop shows which tend to display, the longer they run, a more and more marked tendency to gunplay and brutality. We may ask ourselves, indeed, just what it is that, in the latter case for example, makes the weekly "dose of murder" so attractive. Is it an interest we feel in efficiently-performed police work or is it the chance of a voyeuristic glance into the inner lives of murderers who overstep a boundary we are well aware of – that, namely, which separates us from the forbidden region of our own part of aggressivity and anti-social instinct? Is the fascination, in the end, a fascination with our own shadow? Whatever the answer to these questions, the fact remains that every culture in the world seems to have an appetite for films portraying domination, conflict, murder and subjugation – in short, the darker side of our own selves.

By far the most successful TV series ever, for example – the still-running "Game of Thrones" – is nothing but a grandiose web of murder, love, hate, torture, ambush, treachery, trickery, rape, slaughter and despair. As its title indicates, it is the story of the long and complex contest for the supreme lordship over an imaginary "land of seven kingdoms". It shows heroes and heroines following their respective "wills to power" in a fateful struggle which sees them throw into the balance both their highest talents and their basest instincts. This heroic struggle for power, up to the very limits of the suffering that human beings are capable of, is the theme *par excellence* of all

Mankind's myths and epics. Nietzsche, at bottom, asks only that we face this fact and acknowledge the hunger for power that characterizes our species.

If we deny this will to power and repress our innate drive to master and dominate, we are turning away from our own nature and our destiny. It is nothing less than a "no" spoken to life itself. A human being who foregoes the development of his own will to power and opts to lead his life in terms of empathy, humility, non-violence and brotherly love is, Nietzsche argues, at best just half a human being. We must accept our own impulse toward self-intensification and thus our own will to power, even if this latter appears to have something "demonic" about it:

[...] The love of power is the demon of men. Let them have everything – health, food, a place to live, entertainment – they are and remain unhappy and low-spirited;

for the demon waits and waits and will be satisfied. Take everything from them and satisfy this and they are almost happy – as happy as men and demons can be. [115]

The exercise of power is, indeed, inevitable in the end, inasmuch as the pursuit of our own interests necessarily impinges on the interests of others:

No egoism at all exists that remains within itself and does not encroach [...] [116]

Our egoism – or, as Nietzsche sometimes puts it, our "intensification of our own lives" – belongs to our very nature. It is, therefore, not "evil" even if it proves disadvantageous to others:

I do not count the evil and painful character of existence a reproach to it but hope rather that it will one day be more evil and painful than hitherto. [117]

The will to power, then, is beyond good and evil. But is there a limit to this? Nietzsche flirts, in this passage, with the idea of evil as an intensification of the process of stripping away from ourselves our mechanisms of self-restraint and self-limitation. Far from criticizing human existence because of all that is evil and painful in it, Nietzsche sees that to hope, as he does, that the future will see a greater unfolding of human will and power is tantamount to hoping that this existence will become "more evil and painful than hitherto". Does Nietzsche wish, then, to do away with every kind of morality?

> What is good? – Everything that enhances people's feeling of power, will to power, power itself.

> What is bad? – Everything stemming from weakness. [118]

Nietzsche, indeed, is happy to call himself an "immoralist" and even to evoke the term "Anti-Christ". And it is certainly true that his criticism of traditional moral systems, and of Christianity, as mere "weakness" was a more virulent criticism than had ever before been articulated. And yet he is not to be described as "amoral". His contention is always only that, on our way to becoming higher beings or "overmen", we must free ourselves from older value-systems and learn to give ourselves our own system of values and our own morality:

We [...] want to *become who we are* – human beings who are new, unique, incomparable, who give themselves laws, who create themselves! [119]

The "human being of a new kind", then – or the "overman" – is not amoral but rather only someone who gives moral laws to himself. The overman, indeed, can even be said to be, at bottom, more moral than the Christian, since this latter allows the Ten Commandments and other moral values to be prescribed for him by sources outside his own self:

[...] The measure of his value lies outside him. [120]

What Nietzsche rejects is rather an overarching moral system which denies individualism and prescribes to all men and women indiscriminately ideals of who and how they ought to be:

> A man as he *ought* to be; that sounds to us as insipid as "a tree as it ought to be". [121]

After "the death of God" Man must free himself from slave morality and create his own individual values. Zarathustra thus poses the decisive question:

> Can you give yourself your own evil and good and hang your will above yourself like a law? [122]

Nietzsche hereby thinks modern individualism through to its radical conclusion. Who should morally govern the individual, if not the individual himself? Nietzsche, then, was not amoral. He merely called for a pluralism of values, a pluralism of individual moralities:

> [...] Just as, in certain cases, suns of different colours will shine on a single planet [...] in the same way [...] we modern men are determined by a *diversity* of morals. [123]

But what does "a diversity of morals" imply for our lives together as citizens of states? As a political alternative to democracy, which Nietzsche dismisses as an "institution promoting herd morality" and "the rule of the rabble", he looks back and celebrates the aristocratic societies of the ancient world as the best of all political orders. Nietzsche understood "aristocracy" in its strict etymological sense of "rule by the best". But, conceived in Nietzschean terms, even an aristocratic society would be a somewhat self-contradictory thing. The greatest contradiction here would ensue from Nietzsche's characterization of the overman and of this latter's will to power: how would it be possible for an individual liberated from all externally-imposed values to continue to live in a community with other similarly liberated individuals, since each would obey only his own self-given laws and his own will to power? What happens when two such "overmen" encounter one another as representatives of directly contrary sets of values? The answer which Nietzsche places in the mouth of his Zarathustra is an ambiguous one:

> In this manner sure and beautiful let us also be *enemies*, my friends. Divinely let us struggle *against* each other! [124]

In *The Will to Power*, the collection of unpublished fragments that was presented, after his death, by Nietzsche's sister as his *magnum opus*, we find him expanding somewhat on this view:

> I dream of a brotherhood of men who are unconditional, who give no quarter, and who happily call themselves "destroyers"; they would measure everything against the standard of their critique and even sacrifice their own selves to truth. [125]

From these few hints one can glean that Nietzsche envisaged an anarchistically disputatious society of free individuals who, aware of their radical diversity, would struggle amicably to assert their respective values. Also interesting in this connection is his radical vision of the so-called "criminal of a possible future" who, while giving himself his own laws and acting in accordance with these laws, by the same token makes himself also his own judge:

> Is a state of affairs unthinkable in which the malefactor calls himself to account and publicly dictates his own punishment in the proud feeling that he is thus honouring the law which he himself has made? [126]

This is indeed an interesting vision. But should it turn out to be the case that the criminal of the future does not feel himself to be a "malefactor" at all and appeals only to his "will to power" as do all the other "overmen" around him, then an agreement on shared values that a society might live by is hardly to be expected. At best, there would arise here an anarchy of wishes or a creative chaos; at worst, a war of all against all; and in any case, certainly nothing resembling a "rule of law".

There can be no doubt but that a functioning morality depends – just as much as does a functioning traffic system, with its roadsigns, traffic lights and speed lanes – vitally and essentially upon the fact that it is supported and observed equally by all. There is no more room in such a morality for individually creative private solutions than there is in a traffic system for such "creative acts" as running a red light. This key problem – namely, that a mass of "liberated" higher beings who would create their own values and follow only their respective wills to power – could hardly live together is one that Nietzsche, indeed, sometimes recognizes and admits:

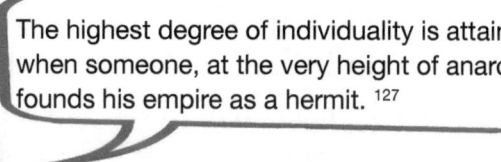

> The highest degree of individuality is attained when someone, at the very height of anarchy, founds his empire as a hermit. [127]

Since, however, we cannot all be hermits, the problem of how "overmen" are to live as a society remains unsolved. In his "Zarathustra" Nietzsche is more consistent and envisages the self-development of the overman as no longer, in principle, occurring within any kind of state or political organism at all, all forms of which he dismisses here as hopelessly "poisoned":

"State" I call it where all are drinkers of poison, the good and the bad; "state" where all lose themselves [...] There, where the state ends, only there begins the human being [...] [128]

There is no doubt: no state can be built on the basis of Nietzsche's ideas. His criticisms of the nationalism that was on the rise in his day, of socialism, democracy, anti-Semitism, Social Darwinism and modern capitalism are all precise and astonishingly far-sighted. But his own political vision of an aristocratic anarchism cannot, in the end, be made a reality. Nietzsche was not a political theorist; but he was all the more brilliant a psychologist for just that reason.

He reminded us that we are not sublimely moral beings of pure intellect or pure spirit but rather beings of instinct afflicted with emotions that harmonize only poorly with existence in society. And our way of dealing with these emotions, he argues, cannot and must not any longer be, as it had been for centuries, a mere suppressing and repressing of them:

> This unnaturalness corresponds to that dualistic conception of a merely good and a merely evil creature [...] The one has a right to exist, the other ought not to be there at all [...] [129]

Instead of the systematic repression of drives and instincts and the false humility of the pious Nietzsche proposes the "free spirit" with his "right to do all he wills". Each one of us, he argues, should find his or her own particular way of dealing responsibly with their own good and evil drives and instincts. This, however, is somethingfor which no sure formula exists:

I want to help all those who are seeking something to pattern themselves on by showing just *how* one seeks a pattern; and

my greatest joy is to encounter individual patterns which do *not* resemble me. May the Devil take all imitators [...]¹³⁰

The Dionysian Life – Trusting One's Feelings

Nietzsche criticizes nothing so harshly as he does Man's hostility to his own body. For thousands of years, the ecstatic, chaotic, creative bodily element – in short, the Donysian aspect of Man – was repressed in favour of Man's rational, logical aspect. This was, and remains, unhealthy.

For this reason, Nietzsche condemns metaphysicians, priests and teachers of religion, who direct people's attention exclusively toward reason and the "pure soul", as "despisers of the body". Sarcastically he advises them to try getting by without a body and see what happens then:

> To the despisers of the body I want to say my words. I do not think they should relearn and teach differently; instead, they should bid their own bodies farewell – and thus fall silent. [131]

After two thousand years of hostility to the body – on the part first of Platonic philosophy, and then of the Judaic as well as the Christian religion in both its Catholic and Protestant forms, all of which taught that the body was sinful and a mere servant of the mind and spirit – Nietzsche was the first to demand that we acknowledge and embrace once again our physicality and our animal origins. His great credo runs:

> Body I am through and through, and nothing besides. [132]

Nietzsche also corrects another error that had lasted for millennia. Some years before Freud he recognized and understood "bad conscience" to be a merely secondary phenomenon, a product of evolution. He saw, in other words, that the human "conscience" was nothing planted by God in Man at his creation but is rather nourished by our own animal energies which we no longer, as we did in prehistoric times, discharge toward the outside world in the form of drives and emotions but now rather turn against ourselves.

And thirdly – and this was perhaps his greatest contribution to depth psychology – Nietzsche called into question the *cogito ergo sum* of Descartes (that is to say, the thinking "I") as the guarantor and governor of our existence. We believe, he argued, that we are acting as *homo sapiens* – that is to say, according to the dictates of our reason – but in reality we follow only the hidden, unconscious will of our body, which is the force, in the end, which always decides:

The body is a great reason [...] Your small reason, what you call "spirit", is also a tool of your body, my brother, a small work- and plaything of your great reason. [133]

In this last-quoted passage Nietzsche completely re-verses the traditional hierarchy of mind (or "spirit") and body. The accepted wisdom had always been: rea-son (mind, spirit) rules and governs the body, since Man is a rational being. But Nietzsche contends the very opposite: it is really the body that is "the great reason" which leads us in all our actions; the intellect, by contrast, is only a "small reason" which is not even able to make decisions for itself. The much-praised "reasoning and deliberating consciousness", then, is merely an illusion in which our human ego is happy to believe. In reality, this consciousness just invents, by hindsight, legitimating reasons for actions that our body has already decided upon and indeed, in most cases, already carried out:

"I" you say and are proud of this word. But what is greater is that in which you do not want to believe – your body and its great reason. It does not say "I" but *does* "I". [134]

Some decades later, this phenomenon – that of the conscious "ego"'s really doing nothing more, though believing itself to be guiding our actions, than providing *ex post facto* justifications for actions already undertaken by the body – was given, by the psychoanalyst Freud, the more precise technical designation: "rationalization". In his famous statement that "the ego is not master in its own house" Freud takes over almost word for word Nietzsche's critique of the rational consciousness.

Nietzsche's significance for that new vision of Man developed by psychoanalysis, and for that new understanding of ourselves which has risen to dominance throughout the 20th Century and our own, has been immense. It is also in this sense that his philosophy can be understood to represent a sea change. He not only predicted the rise of what he called "European nihilism", with its various aberrations in the form of nationalism, socialism and capitalism; he also clearly recognized that Man is not – as such philosophers of the Enlightenment as Descartes, Hume and Kant had contended he was – a being governed purely by reason or understanding. Man, argued Nietzsche, is and will forever remain a being of drives and instincts, whose life draws and depends, necessarily, on his unconscious Dionysian wishes and needs:

It is here I set the Dionysus of the Greeks: the [...] affirmation of life, life whole and not denied or in part. [135]

But of what use is Nietzsche's judgment to us today? As Nietzsche sees it, our culture has become thoroughly ossified within its corset of logical thinking. It has reached such a point that this culture now demands logical justifications for absolutely everything. We are caught in a kind of dictatorship of rational thought. The ordering and form-giving principle in Man appears to have prevailed. Notwithstanding this, however, ecstatic, creative forces still stir within every human being. Nietzsche urges us to allow free rein to these forces whose effects have hitherto been kept confined within the realm of the sub-conscious. Because anyone who represses too strictly these Dionysian impulses within himself runs the risk of becoming sick:

For what does one have to atone most? For one's modesty; for having failed to listen to one's most personal requirements [...] This lack of reverence for oneself avenges itself through every kind of deprivation: health, friendship, wellbeing, pride, cheerfulness, freedom, firmness, courage. [136]

Following Nietzsche, Freud later urged his patients not to be swayed by moral considerations into repressing too many of their lives' strongly-felt wishes if they do not wish to fall ill from this "life unlived". "All those," he wrote, "who wish to be more noble-minded than their constitution allows fall victim to neurosis."[137] Nietzsche had formulated the same idea differently a few decades earlier:

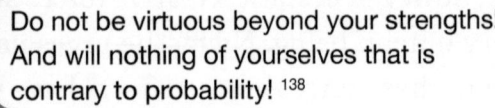

Do not be virtuous beyond your strengths! And will nothing of yourselves that is contrary to probability! [138]

For both Nietzsche and Freud, to live a healthy life means to live a life as joyful as possible and to develop one's deeply rooted personal potential. Out of this insight Freud developed a form of therapy which freed individuals from inhibitions of all sorts: from past traumatizing experiences, through pangs of conscience arising from the super-ego, through to the pain of "lives unlived". But can we profit from Nietzsche's urging of a Dionysian style of life beyond its inspiring of certain therapeutic techniques? Is it practically possible to live this way? Must we not all of us necessarily comply with our culture's sexual morality and with social norms?

It may indeed do one good, psychologically, to live out all one's impulses of anger: for example, to tell one's boss what one thinks of him and throw up one's job. It is certainly tempting to follow no path but that which one's feelings, intuitions and desire for pleasure prompt one to take. But (as Nietzsche himself concedes) such choices can amount, in many cases, not just to a transgression of social rules but can also hurt and anger other people. People who "live in a Dionysian manner" are often a great strain upon those around them. One need only think of the trail of broken female hearts that a "Don Juan" figure leaves behind him or of the countless broken homes that ensue when men – who, evolutionary biology tells us, tend in any case rather to polygamy – decide to live out their "Dionysian aspects". One might also consider the unforeseeable consequences of all the acts of aggression and vengeance carried out in such states of "being outside of oneself".

Nietzsche, of course, when he urges us to live "Dionysian lives", means much more than just that we should resolutely live out the sensual aspects of our personality. What he envisages is a general "intensification of life", a passionate development of our "higher selves":

Everyone has his good days when he discovers his higher self; and true humanity demands that everyone be evaluated only in the light of this condition [...] A painter, for example, should be appraised and revered in the light of the highest vision he is capable of seeing and reproducing. [139]

Thus, the painter Van Gogh, for example, trusted only this "higher self" and his own Dionysian vision. Drawing on his own deepest feelings, he painted in an expressionistic style which met with little or no understanding among his contemporaries and attained global fame only years after his death. Van Gogh himself remained unknown in his lifetime and died in poverty, although today his paintings are sold for the highest prices in the world. Nietzsche was a similar case. His brief professorial tenure at the University of Basel, from which illness forced him to retire at the early age of thirty-five, provided him with a small pension but the many books he published sold so badly that he had to finance their publication himself. He began to acquire a small number of devoted readers only in the last few years of his active life although, ironically, in the ten years between his total mental breakdown in 1889 and his death in 1900 he acquired the fame that had eluded him all his active life. A certain independence, however, from the recognition and the opinion of others is, for Nietzsche, one of the three key characteristics of the great man who trusts only to his own nature:

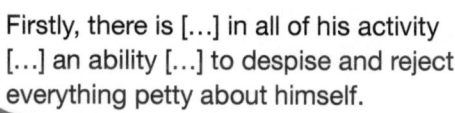

Firstly, there is [...] in all of his activity [...] an ability [...] to despise and reject everything petty about himself.

> Secondly, he is colder, harder, less hesitating and without fear of "opinion" [...] Thirdly, he knows he is incommunicable [...] There is a solitude within him [...] his own justice that is beyond appeal. [140]

Although Nietzsche's vision of the new Dionysian man seems tailored specifically to the figure of the artist, unfolding his inner potential outside of all social constraints, those of us who are not artists can also gain much from these exhortations. Above all today, when we all live in a world which is overly intellectualized and in which the omnipresent media impose a tremendous pressure to conform, it can be extremely liberating to give a freer rein once again to one's own intuitions.

Become Who You Are! The Three Steps on the Path to the Overman

Few words are used more frequently by Nietzsche than the word "dare". He urges us to leave the safe harbour of our habits, our morality and our mediocrity with a view to unchaining our noblest drives and impulses:

We, however, want to *become who we are* – human beings who [...] create themselves! [141]

In order to develop this our highest creative potential we must, at a certain point in our lives, cross the threshold to our hidden essence. But how does one reach this threshold? Nietzsche's "prophet", Zarathustra, answers this question, right at the start of the book that bears his name, in what has now become a famous parable:

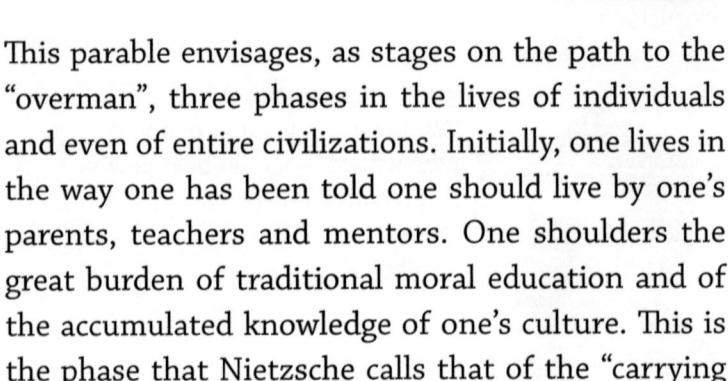

Three metamorphoses of the spirit I name for you: how the spirit becomes a camel, and the camel a lion, and finally the lion a child. [142]

This parable envisages, as stages on the path to the "overman", three phases in the lives of individuals and even of entire civilizations. Initially, one lives in the way one has been told one should live by one's parents, teachers and mentors. One shoulders the great burden of traditional moral education and of the accumulated knowledge of one's culture. This is the phase that Nietzsche calls that of the "carrying spirit", which resembles a patient, obedient camel:

[...] The carrying spirit [...] kneels down like a camel and wants to be well loaded. [143]

The camel here also stands as an allegory for that spirit which bears the tutelage, restriction and oppression by the church which weighed on European humanity for thousands of years. At a certain point, however, this camel "metamorphoses" into a fighting lion and tears apart all the moral restraints placed on him by education and society. This is the phase of dawning individual or cultural adulthood and self-liberation. Whereas the camel had still hearkened to all the old "thou shalt"s and "thou shalt not"s, the lion's dictum is: "I do as I will..." The lion, then, stands for the collapse of the old moral values and for a dawning of absolute freedom which is also the rise of what Nietzsche calls "nihilism". The lion, in other words, is the great (self-)liberator from all that is old and traditional; but he is not yet able to establish new values of his own:

To create new values – not even the lion is capable of that. But to create freedom for itself for new creation – that is within the power of the lion. [144]

This blow for freedom that is struck by the lion is an extremely important step within both the history of an individual and that of a culture. But it is by no means the final goal. Because, as we have said, the dawn of freedom tends also to mean the dawn of nihilism: of a loss of belief in any and every value. And this too needs to be overcome. Nihilism, for Nietzsche, must not be a state into which mankind settles complacently down. There are many people, he says, who can talk for hours about all that they have liberated themselves from, all that they have left behind them. But, says Nietzsche, merely to be "free *from*" something is not enough:

> Your dominating thought I want to hear, and not that you escaped from a yoke [...] Free from what? What does Zarathustra care? But brightly your eyes should signal to me: free *for* what? [145]

The important thing, in other words, is the forward path that we decide upon and what we do with our hard-won freedom. One might say that Nietzsche's own life provides an illustration of these three phases. Son of a Lutheran pastor who died when Nietzsche was only five, he spent the first phase of his life being raised, by women alone, according to strict Pietistic principles, and this phase was prolonged beyond the threshold of manhood by his years at the equally strict elite boarding school Schulpforta which he left only at the age of almost twenty. This "phase of the camel" ended, however, and the "phase of the lion" began when, at the age of twenty-one, as a student in Leipzig, he stumbled on a copy of Schopenhauer's *World As Will and Idea* in a second-hand bookshop. Devouring Schopenhauer's *magnum opus* at a gulp, he freed himself from the bonds of his former piety and became Christianity's harshest critic. In the years that followed he fought free, in-deed, of every kind of metaphysical "philosophy of the spirit", including Schopenhauer's own, which he soon came to recognize as after all only a variant of Christian religiosity. But it was only in a third phase of his life – which began properly only with his own poetic *magnum opus, Thus Spoke Zarathustra* and with his vision of the overman – that he dared to trust to his own thought and to develop a vision all his own. In the parable we have cited Nietzsche calls this third phase the phase of the metamorphosis of the lion into a child at play:

But tell me, my brothers, of what is the child capable that even the lion is not? [146]

This transformation of the lion into a child at play is surely the most striking of all the images that Nietzsche offers us in his description of the path leading to the "higher man" – perhaps because the expected image in this third and most decisive phase of the metamorphosis into the overman proper might rather have been that of some mighty, vigorous beast or some invincible mythical being, or in any case something quite other than a mere child at play.

The meaning of this last metamorphosis is, however, immediately intuitively clear. Only a child at play has within himself that potential of the "higher man" which is now most needed and most decisive. He is free from all old ballast, innocent, inquisitive, lively, full of a thirst for action, and as yet entirely unspoilt:

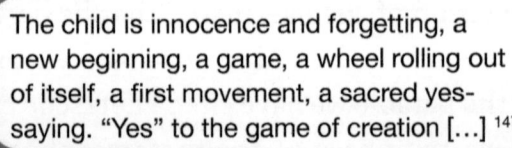

The child is innocence and forgetting, a new beginning, a game, a wheel rolling out of itself, a first movement, a sacred yes-saying. "Yes" to the game of creation [...] [147]

The child at play is the finale of a story of emancipation, a "coming out" after the shaking off of old burdens. The painter Picasso, who struggled all his life to attain to his new abstract form of artistic self-expression, uses a similar metaphor to describe his liberation from the yoke of the traditional style of painting: "One needs a long time to become young".

Just this is Nietzsche's message to us also. It requires much time for us to become so young that we can approach the world once again, unburdened by old ballast, as a child at play approaches it:

Human maturity: this means rediscovering the seriousness we had toward play when we were children. [148]

But of what use is this thought of Nietzsche's to us today? Does each of us really pass through these three phases of the "camel", the "lion" and the "child at play"? Does there exist even in the life of a perfect-ly normal individual the chance, at a certain point, of "becoming young again"? Might the famous "mid-life crisis" be such a point: a point at which one can shake off old responsibilities and re-invent oneself? Is Nietzsche thinking perhaps of the middle-aged husband and father who, once the kids have gone off to college, suddenly quits his job and rides around the world on a Harley-Davidson? No. In his highly poetic language Nietzsche is asking much more of us:

> Are you a new strength and a new right? A first movement? A wheel rolling out of itself? Can you compel even the stars to revolve around you? [149]

What Nietzsche is concerned with, then, is more than just a belated turn to hedonism or a change of career. The path to becoming a "higher kind of human being" is an existential act of self-intensification. In the "child at play" the human spirit becomes that which it really is and can be – it becomes free. It is now able to decide itself which direction its life will take.

If one sums up all the characteristics that Nietzsche ascribes to his overman we may say that this overman is at the same time an inquisitive child at play and a creative being who remains, passionately but without vanity, obligated and devoted to his own highest goal and purpose. But this creative being also pursues his will to power. Once he has identified this highest goal and purpose, he will be willing to make every sacrifice in its service and to proceed harshly both with himself and with others in order to attain it.

But what does this mean for us? Can a normal human being follow this path toward the overman and carry through this triple metamorphosis from "camel" into "lion" and from "lion" into "child at play"? Nietzsche's appeal, as he himself writes, is directed to all those who wish to hear him. But the taking of the path out of slavery into free self-development has one very prosaic but nonetheless important precondition: namely, time:

As at all times, so now too, men are divided into the slaves and the free. For he who does not have two thirds of his day to himself is a slave, let him be what he may otherwise be: statesman, businessman, official, scholar. [150]

One great necessary precondition, then, for the development of one's creative potential is having time to feel this potential within oneself and to actualize it. After an eight-hour working day much potential necessarily remains unactualized. In France many jobs involve only a six-hour working day – which would mean that, if one were able to get by with relatively little sleep, the condition set by Nietzsche of "two thirds of the day" free to be devoted to self-development would indeed be fulfilled. May we say, then, that French people, or anybody who can afford to work only part-time, have a greater chance of "Dionysian" self-fulfillment than the rest of us? And, above all: is this intensification of one's own existence a path reserved for artists, writers, poets, painters, composers etc., or can, for example, an unmarried mother raising her child alone be on the way to becoming such a "higher being"? Does she too not have a noble goal and purpose for the sake of which she has left her old world behind and for which she is prepared to make great sacrifices?

There can be no doubt but that such a single mother embodies many of the characteristics which Nietzsche specifies to be those of the overman. If such a woman intuitively meets, in "Dionysian" manner, the challenge of bringing a child into the world; gives up completely, in a second phase, her former life as a young woman without family commitments, liberating herself from all social conventions and resistances; and then, in a third phase, pulls off the balancing act of playing also the paternal role for her child, giving him or her a sense both of love and security, without thereby being too "smothering" – it is impossible to deny that all this amounts to an enormous achievement of the human will. As in the case of many great artists, this achievement usually remains without social recognition. This too, however, fits the quality of a total absence of vanity which Nietzsche repeatedly emphatically ascribes to the overman and goes to support the contention that the achievement such a single mother can lay claim to is indeed equivalent to that which Nietzsche cites as the achievement of a "superior human being".

A single mother – an "overman" on a par with Goethe, Napoleon or Van Gogh? Can one, then, really interpret Nietzsche's vision of a higher, nobler form of human being as an urging of us all to develop those noblest parts of our own potential?

One repays a teacher badly if one always remains a pupil only.[151]

Say "Yes" to Life – Embrace Life's Joys and Also Its Sorrows!

Of what use is Nietzsche's central idea to us today? In the last analysis, what he wants to say to us with his philosophy is something very simple. Life – everyone's life – involves suffering. There is no human being anywhere whom suffering does not, in some form, touch – who does not at some point feel lonely or abandoned, or loses a loved one, or fails in some enterprise, or does harm to themselves or others, or suffers a personal defeat, or is plagued by illness or merely by the approach of old age. Even the children who give us such joy when they are small can cause us an equal amout of suffering as they grow up. There can be no doubt: to live is to suffer.

This insight – uncontestable but nonetheless profound – is one that Nietzsche shares with the writer who set him on the path toward philosophy: Schopenhauer. But he draws conclusions from this insight that are much more radical than those drawn by his mentor. Even in the face of suffering, says Nietzsche, we must never say "no" to life. Instead of retreating into meditation, ascetic exercises or the contemplation of art, as Schopenhauer (inspired in part by Buddhism for which he professed great admiration) urges us to do, Nietzsche demands of us that we shoulder a far greater task. We must, he says, learn to take life in its entirety. And our "stomach", as he puts it, is fully capable of digesting all that life presents it with:

> *Courage to suffer.-* As we are now, we are able to endure a fairly large amount of unpleasure, and our stomach is designed to take this heavy fare. Perhaps without it we would find life's repast insipid; and without our ready tolerance of pain we would have to give up too many pleasures! [152]

Nietzsche urges on us here a "will to pain" and a "courage to suffer", because both are essential parts of human existence. We have seen that already in the tragedies of classical Greece the hero was shown struggling against overwhelmingly powerful foes and suffering countless torments. But despite this – or rather precisely because of this – he remains a hero. Every individual, Nietzsche tells us, bears the qualities of a hero within themselves and should live these qualities out:

Yes, my friends, believe as I do in Dionysian life and in the rebirth of tragedy. The time of Socratic Man is past [...] Now you must only dare to be tragic human beings [...] [153]

We must become tragic human beings. Nietzsche's Dionysian approach to suffering – which he conceives of not, as Christianity does, as a punishment but, on the contrary, as a distinction – was summed up by no one so succinctly as by that great German poet with whom Nietzsche was, in so many things, of one mind: Goethe. In a well-known poem Goethe writes:

"All things the gods bestow, the infinite gods,

Upon on their favoured ones, completely.

All joys they bestow, all the infinite joys,

And all sorrows as well, all the infinite sorrows,

Upon their favoured ones, completely."

To say "yes" to life, then, means to accept the pains and sorrows, great and small, that life brings with it, because joy and sorrow are indivisibly linked:

Pain is also a joy, a curse is also a blessing, night is also a sun [...] Have you ever said "yes" to one joy? O my friends, then you also said "yes" to *all* pain. All things are enchained, entwined, enamoured. [154]

But if all things are indivisibly enchained and entwined with one another, one cannot, if one is consistent, want only to enjoy life's pleasurable side over and over again; one must also say an unconditional "yes" to the more sombre things in life:

[...] love it eternally and for all time; and say to pain also: refrain, but come back! [155]

If we succeed in doing this we will be rewarded for it. We often emerge fortified from painful experiences. It was perhaps such experiences that inspired Nietzsche to one of his most frequently quoted philosophical formulations:

What doesn't kill me makes me stronger. [156]

It is no wonder that this dictum of Nietzsche's is so often cited, nowadays mostly with a wink of irony, by people all over the world when their plans have gone awry or they have come face to face with some painful aspect of life. In view of the many psychological and physical injuries each of us suffers each day, the question does indeed arise of just where we find the resolution that we need to tackle life day after day in what Nietzsche calls the tragic, Dionysian spirit:

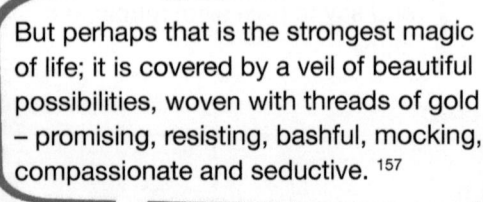

But perhaps that is the strongest magic of life; it is covered by a veil of beautiful possibilities, woven with threads of gold – promising, resisting, bashful, mocking, compassionate and seductive. [157]

Life's magic itself, then, seduces us into going on and provides new nourishment for our will to create:

Creating – that is the great redemption from suffering, and life's becoming light. But in order for the creator to be, suffering is needed and much transformation. [158]

Through acts of creation we can free ourselves, to an extent, from suffering. Thus, many people speak enthusiastically about the so-called "flow": an exalted state in which one feels completely absorbed and borne along by one's work. But creativity too, says Nietzsche, rests upon a foundation of transformation and suffering. Life, in its essential profundity, requires everything at once: transformation, pain and joy, as a constant process of ascent and descent:

"*The world is deep*
And deeper than the grasp of day.
Deep is its pain.
Joy, deeper still than misery.
Pain says: refrain!
Yet all joy wants eternity,
Wants deep, wants deep eternity!" [159]

Nietzsche is the great representative of what has been called "the philosophy of life". Although, as a philosopher and psychologist, he displays a keener insight than anyone before or since into the weaknesses and failings of human beings – our vanity, our resentments and our worship of false gods and idols – he declares himself, nevertheless, unconditionally on the side of life. And although he lived, himself, a retired and solitary life, devoting himself to the writing of his many books, he made himself the great defender, among philosophers, of sensuality, bodily experience, and the unfolding of one's inner Dionysian aspirations. The great legacy that he has left to us is his passionate appeal that we free ourselves from the bonds and restrictions of rationalism. It is not reason, or intellect, or logically ordering and classifying thought alone that we must allow to become the sole helmsman of our existence. A key role here must always be played also by that child who continues to live within us all:

[...] one must still have chaos in oneself in order to give birth to a dancing star. [160]

Bibliographical References

There currently exists no single "standard edition" of Nietzsche's works in English but Cambridge University Press has published, in the course of the past thirty years, new English editions of all those works which Nietzsche himself published, in German, in his lifetime. Most of the quotations from Nietzsche given here follow the text of these Cambridge University Press editions.

It is only with regard to the large body of writing left unpublished when Nietzsche lost his reason in 1889 that a non-Cambridge text is sometimes cited here. Cambridge University Press, indeed, has published a volume drawing on these unpublished writings of the 1880s (Writings from the Late Notebooks, edited by Ruediger Bittner, 2003). But, influenced by recent critical controversies, this volume is very selective. A wider selection of the late, unpublished writings is offered by the volume The Will to Power, the subject of many dozens of re-editions and translations into various languages since its initial publication, one year after Nietzsche's death, in 1901. The Will to Power has been the object of harsh criticism by some modern Nietzsche scholars but their rejection of it is rather the rejection of the claim – put forward by its original editor and publisher, Nietzsche's sister Elisabeth – that it is a work of Nietzsche's and indeed his major work. This it is not. But few scholars contest that the notes which Elisabeth used to assemble it were indeed authored by Nietzsche. For the many passages that Walther Ziegler cites from the "late notebooks", then, the 1967 English-language edition of The Will to Power has been used.

1   Friedrich Nietzsche, Thus Spoke Zarathustra (edited by Adrian del Caro and Robert Pippin), Cambridge University Press, 2006, p. 59 (On the Bestowing Virtue).
2   Friedrich Nietzsche, The Gay Science (edited by Bernard Williams), Cambridge University Press, 2001, p. 120 (The Madman).
3   Friedrich Nietzsche, The Will To Power (edited by Walter Kaufmann), Vintage Books, New York, 1967, p. 3.
4   Friedrich Nietzsche, The Gay Science (edited by Bernard Williams), Cambridge University Press, 2001, p. 120 (The Madman).

5   Ibid.
6   Friedrich Nietzsche, Human, All Too Human,
    Cambridge University Press, 1986, p. 25.
7   Friedrich Nietzsche, The Will To Power (ed. Walter Kaufmann),
    Vintage Books, New York, 1967, p. 395.
8   Friedrich Nietzsche, Daybreak (ed. Clark, Leiter),
    Cambridge University Press, 1997, p. 176.
9   Friedrich Nietzsche, The Anti-Christ and Other Writings
    (ed. Aaron Ridley and Judith Norman), Cambridge University Press,
    2005 p. 157.
10 Friedrich Nietzsche, The Will To Power (ed. Walter Kaufmann),
    Vintage Books, New York, 1967, p. 460.
11 Nietzsche's late notes remain, as remarked above, only partially
    translated into English and this passage appears to be one of the
    passages from Nietzsche's unpublished notes that has "fallen through
    the cracks" in the controversial history of Nietzsche's translation and
    publication. The translation, then, is my own. The original German
    text is to be found in the Montinari and Colli edition (KSA, 12, 7 [67])
12 Friedrich Nietzsche, Human, All Too Human, Cambridge University
    Press, 1986, pp. 173-174.
13 Friedrich Nietzsche, Daybreak (ed. Clark, Leiter), Cambridge
    University Press, 1997, p. 106.
14 Friedrich Nietzsche, The Anti-Christ and Other Writings
    (ed. Aaron Ridley and Judith Norman), Cambridge University Press,
    2005, pp. 214-215.
15 Friedrich Nietzsche, The Gay Science (edited by Bernard Williams),
    Cambridge University Press, 2001, p. 120 (The Madman).
16 Friedrich Nietzsche, Thus Spoke Zarathustra (edited by Adrian del
    Caro and Robert Pippin), Cambridge University Press, 2006, p. 59
    (On the Bestowing Virtue).
17 Ibid. pp. 5-6.
18 Ibid. p. 7
19 Ibid. p. 192.
20 Friedrich Nietzsche, The Will To Power (ed. Walter Kaufmann),
    Vintage Books, New York, 1967, p. 550.
21 Ibid. p. 542
22 Ibid. p. 191

23 Friedrich Nietzsche, The Anti-Christ and Other Writings
    (ed. Aaron Ridley and Judith Norman), Cambridge University Press,
    2005, p. 4
24 Friedrich Nietzsche, The Will To Power (ed. Walter Kaufmann),
    Vintage Books, New York, 1967, pp. 419-20.
25 Friedrich Nietzsche, The Birth of Tragedy and Other Writings
    (ed. Geuss and Speirs), Cambridge University Press 1999, p. 113
26 Ibid. p. 114
27 Friedrich Nietzsche, The Anti-Christ and Other Writings
    (ed. Aaron Ridley and Judith Norman), Cambridge University Press,
    2005, p. 166
28 Ibid.
29 Friedrich Nietzsche, The Birth of Tragedy and Other Writings
    (ed. Geuss and Speirs), Cambridge University Press 1999, p. 98
30 Friedrich Nietzsche, On the Genealogy of Morality
    (ed. Ansell-Pearson), Cambridge University Press 2006, p. 17
31 Ibid. p. 32.
32 Friedrich Nietzsche, The Will To Power (ed. Walter Kaufmann),
    Vintage Books, New York, 1967, p. 468.
33 Friedrich Nietzsche, The Anti-Christ and Other Writings
    (ed. Aaron Ridley and Judith Norman), Cambridge University Press,
    2005, p. 65.
34 Friedrich Nietzsche, The Will To Power (ed. Walter Kaufmann),
    Vintage Books, New York, 1967, p. 199.
35 Ibid.
36 Friedrich Nietzsche, Daybreak (ed. Clark and Leiter), Cambridge
    University Press, 1997, p. 109.
37 Friedrich Nietzsche, The Will To Power (ed. Walter Kaufmann),
    Vintage Books, New York, 1967, pp. 192-93.
38 Again, this appears to be one of the passages from Nietzsche's late
    unpublished notes that has "fallen through the cracks" in the
    controversial history of Nietzsche's translation and publication.
    The translation is my own. The German original is to be found under
    eKGWB/NF-1885,36[16] in the online digital edition of Colli and
    Montinari's Complete Critical Edition..
39 Friedrich Nietzsche, The Will To Power (ed. Walter Kaufmann),
    Vintage Books, New York, 1967, p. 543.

40   Friedrich Nietzsche, Human, All Too Human (ed. Schacht), Cambridge University Press, 1986, p. 331.

41   Friedrich Nietzsche, Thus Spoke Zarathustra (edited by Adrian del Caro and Robert Pippin), Cambridge University Press, 2006, p. 6.

42   Friedrich Nietzsche, On the Genealogy of Morality (ed. Ansell-Pearson), Cambridge University Press 2006, p. 56.

43   Ibid.

44   Ibid. p. 57

45   Ibid.

46   Ibid.

47   Ibid.

48   Ibid. (translation slightly revised)

49   Ibid.

50   Ibid.

51   Ibid.

52   Friedrich Nietzsche, The Will To Power (ed. Walter Kaufmann), Vintage Books, New York, 1967, p. 166.

53   Friedrich Nietzsche, Human, All Too Human, Cambridge University Press, 1986, p. 323.

54   Friedrich Nietzsche, On Truth and Lying in an Extra-Moral Sense, in Sander L. Gilman (ed.) Friedrich Nietzsche on Rhetoric and Language, Oxford University Press, 1989, pp. 246-247.

55   Ibid. p. 248.

56   Ibid. p. 247

57   Ibid. p. 249 (translation slightly revised).

58   Ibid.

59   Ibid. pp. 248 and 251

60   Ibid. p.250

61   Ibid. pp. 252-253

62   Ibid. p. 250.

63   Ibid.

64   Friedrich Nietzsche, Human, All Too Human, Cambridge University Press, 1986, p. 16.

65   Friedrich Nietzsche, On Truth and Lying in an Extra-Moral Sense, in Sander L. Gilman (ed.) Friedrich Nietzsche on Rhetoric and Language, Oxford University Press, 1989, pp. 252-254

66   Friedrich Nietzsche, The Will To Power (ed. Walter Kaufmann), Vintage Books, New York, 1967, p. 356

67 Ibid. p. 550.
68 Ibid. p. 367.
69 Ibid. p. 368.
70 Ibid. p. 336
71 Ibid. p. 346.
72 Ibid. p. 368
73 Ibid. p. 349
74 Ibid. p. 344
75 Ibid. p. 199
76 Ibid.
77 Friedrich Nietzsche, Human, All Too Human, Cambridge University Press, 1986, p. 250.
78 Friedrich Nietzsche, The Anti-Christ and Other Writings (ed. Aaron Ridley and Judith Norman), Cambridge University Press, 2005, p. 213.
79 Ibid. p. 214.
80 Ibid. p. 5
81 Friedrich Nietzsche, Human, All Too Human, Cambridge University Press, 1986, p. 113.
82 Friedrich Nietzsche, The Will To Power (ed. Walter Kaufmann), Vintage Books, New York, 1967, p. 206.
83 Ibid. p. 19.
84 Helmut Schmidt, in Giovanni di Lorenzo, Conversation with the Former German Chancellor Helmut Schmidt About His Experience of Moral Extremes, in Die Zeit (Hamburg) 30.08.2007.
85 Ibid.
86 Friedrich Nietzsche, Human, All Too Human, Cambridge University Press, 1986, p. 176.
87 Ibid.
88 Friedrich Nietzsche, On the Genealogy of Morality (ed. Ansell-Pearson), Cambridge University Press 2006, p. 23.
89 Friedrich Nietzsche, Thus Spoke Zarathustra (edited by Adrian del Caro and Robert Pippin), Cambridge University Press, 2006, p. 168 (On Old and New Tables).
90 Friedrich Nietzsche, The Gay Science (edited by Bernard Williams), Cambridge University Press, 2001, p. 242.
91 Ibid. p. 206

92 Friedrich Nietzsche, Daybreak (ed. Clark and Leiter), Cambridge
    University Press, 1997, p. 373
93 Friedrich Nietzsche, Thus Spoke Zarathustra (edited by Adrian del
    Caro and Robert Pippin), Cambridge University Press, 2006, p. 59
    (On the Bestowing Virtue).
94 Friedrich Nietzsche, The Will To Power (ed. Walter Kaufmann),
    Vintage Books, New York, 1967, p. 477.
95 Friedrich Nietzsche, The Gay Science (edited by Bernard Williams),
    Cambridge University Press, 2001, p. 161
96 Friedrich Nietzsche, The Will To Power (ed. Walter Kaufmann),
    Vintage Books, New York, 1967, p. 209.
97 Friedrich Nietzsche, Thus Spoke Zarathustra (edited by Adrian del
    Caro and Robert Pippin), Cambridge University Press, 2006, p. 89
    (On Self-Overcoming).
98 Friedrich Nietzsche, The Will To Power (ed. Walter Kaufmann),
    Vintage Books, New York, 1967, p. 364.
99 Friedrich Nietzsche, The Anti-Christ and Other Writings
    (ed. Aaron Ridley and Judith Norman), Cambridge University Press,
    2005, p. 5.
100 Friedrich Nietzsche, Thus Spoke Zarathustra (edited by Adrian del
    Caro and Robert Pippin), Cambridge University Press, 2006, p. 233
    (On the Higher Man).
101 Friedrich Nietzsche, The Will To Power (ed. Walter Kaufmann),
    Vintage Books, New York, 1967, p. 468.
102 Friedrich Nietzsche, Thus Spoke Zarathustra (edited by Adrian del
    Caro and Robert Pippin), Cambridge University Press, 2006, p. 35
    (On the New Idol).
103 Friedrich Nietzsche, The Anti-Christ and Other Writings
    (ed. Aaron Ridley and Judith Norman), Cambridge University Press,
    2005, p. 157.
104 Friedrich Nietzsche, Daybreak (ed. Clark and Leiter),
    Cambridge University Press, 1997, p. 173.
105 Friedrich Nietzsche, The Anti-Christ and Other Writings
    (ed. Aaron Ridley and Judith Norman), Cambridge University Press,
    2005, p. 99.
106 Ibid. p. 6.
107 Friedrich Nietzsche, The Will To Power (ed. Walter Kaufmann),
    Vintage Books, New York, 1967, p. 36.

108 Friedrich Nietzsche, The Anti-Christ and Other Writings
   (ed. Aaron Ridley and Judith Norman), Cambridge University Press,
   2005, p. 5

109 These remarks, and those in the immediately following passage,
   once again belong to that part of Nietzsche's legacy of unpublished
   notes that has not yet been translated into English. The German
   original is to be found in the Montinari /
   Colli edition at NF 1881 11 [84]

110 See Montinari / Colli edition NF 1886 5 [71].

111 Friedrich Nietzsche, The Will To Power (ed. Walter Kaufmann),
   Vintage Books, New York, 1967, p. 550.

112 Ibid. p. 550.

113 Friedrich Nietzsche, Thus Spoke Zarathustra (edited by Adrian del
   Caro and Robert Pippin), Cambridge University Press, 2006,
   pp. 161-162 (On Old and New Tablets).

114 Ibid. p. 176.

115 Friedrich Nietzsche, Daybreak (ed. Clark and Leiter), Cambridge
   University Press, 1997, p. 146.

116 Friedrich Nietzsche, The Will To Power (ed. Walter Kaufmann),
   Vintage Books, New York, 1967, p. 199.

117 Ibid. p. 206.

118 Friedrich Nietzsche, The Anti-Christ and Other Writings
   (ed. Aaron Ridley and Judith Norman), Cambridge University Press,
   2005, p. 4.

119 Friedrich Nietzsche, The Gay Science (edited by Bernard Williams),
   Cambridge University Press, 2001, p. 189.

120 Friedrich Nietzsche, The Will To Power (ed. Walter Kaufmann),
   Vintage Books, New York, 1967, p. 206.

121 Ibid. p. 181.

122 Friedrich Nietzsche, Thus Spoke Zarathustra (edited by Adrian del
   Caro and Robert Pippin), Cambridge University Press, 2006, p. 46
   (On the Way of the Creator).

123 Friedrich Nietzsche, Beyond Good and Evil (ed. by Rolf-Peter
   Horstmann and Judith Norman) Cambridge University Press, 2002,
   p. 110.

124 Friedrich Nietzsche, Thus Spoke Zarathustra (edited by Adrian del
   Caro and Robert Pippin), Cambridge University Press, 2006, p. 78
   (On the Tarantulas).

125 Again, these remarks belong to that part of Nietzsche's legacy of
    unpublished notes that has not yet been translated into English.
    The German original is to be found in the Montinari /
    Colli edition at NF 1875 5 [30]
126 Friedrich Nietzsche, Daybreak (ed. Clark and Leiter),
    Cambridge University Press, 1997, p. 187.
127 Again, this remark belongs to that part of Nietzsche's legacy of
    unpublished notes that has not yet been translated into English.
    The German original is to be found in the Montinari / Colli edition
    at NF 1880 6 [60]
128 Friedrich Nietzsche, Thus Spoke Zarathustra (edited by Adrian del
    Caro and Robert Pippin), Cambridge University Press, 2006,
    pp. 35-36 (On the New Idol).
129 Friedrich Nietzsche, The Will To Power (ed. Walter Kaufmann),
    Vintage Books, New York, 1967, p. 192.
130 Again, this remark belongs to that part of Nietzsche's legacy of
    unpublished notes that has not yet been translated into English.
    The German original is to be found in the Montinari / Colli edition
    at NF 1880 6 [50]
131 Friedrich Nietzsche, Thus Spoke Zarathustra (edited by Adrian del
    Caro and Robert Pippin), Cambridge University Press, 2006, p. 22
    (On the Despisers of the Body).
132 Ibid. p. 23
133 Ibid.
134 Ibid.
135 Friedrich Nietzsche, The Will To Power (ed. Walter Kaufmann),
    Vintage Books, New York, 1967, p. 542.
136 Ibid. p. 486.
137 Sigmund Freud, Standard Edition, Volume 9, p. 191.
    (Civilized Sexuality and Modern Nervous Illness)
138 Friedrich Nietzsche, Thus Spoke Zarathustra (edited by Adrian del
    Caro and Robert Pippin), Cambridge University Press, 2006, p. 22
    (On the Higher Man).
139 Friedrich Nietzsche, Human, All Too Human, Cambridge University
    Press, 1986, p. 197.
140 Friedrich Nietzsche, The Will To Power (ed. Walter Kaufmann),
    Vintage Books, New York, 1967, p. 505.
141 Friedrich Nietzsche, The Gay Science (edited by Bernard Williams),
    Cambridge University Press, 2001, p. 189.

142 Friedrich Nietzsche, Thus Spoke Zarathustra (edited by Adrian del Caro and Robert Pippin), Cambridge University Press, 2006, p. 16 (On the Three Metamorphoses).

143 Ibid.

144 Ibid. p. 17.

145 Ibid. p. 46

146 Ibid. p. 17.

147 Ibid. p. (translation slightly revised)

148 Friedrich Nietzsche, Beyond Good and Evil (ed. by Rolf-Peter Horstmann and Judith Norman) Cambridge University Press, 2002, p. 62.

149 Friedrich Nietzsche, Thus Spoke Zarathustra (edited by Adrian del Caro and Robert Pippin), Cambridge University Press, 2006, p. 46 (On the Way of the Creator).

150 Friedrich Nietzsche, Human, All Too Human, Cambridge University Press, 1986, p. 132.

151 Friedrich Nietzsche, Thus Spoke Zarathustra (edited by Adrian del Caro and Robert Pippin), Cambridge University Press, 2006, p. 59 (On the Bestowing Virtue).

152 Friedrich Nietzsche, Daybreak (ed. Clark and Leiter), Cambridge University Press, 1997, p. 187.

153 Friedrich Nietzsche, The Birth of Tragedy and Other Writings (ed. Geuss and Speirs), Cambridge University Press 1999, p. 98

154 Friedrich Nietzsche, Thus Spoke Zarathustra (edited by Adrian del Caro and Robert Pippin), Cambridge University Press, 2006, p. 263 (The Sleepwalker Song).

155 Ibid.

156 Friedrich Nietzsche, The Anti-Christ and Other Writings (ed. Aaron Ridley and Judith Norman), Cambridge University Press, 2005, p. 157.

157 Friedrich Nietzsche, The Gay Science (edited by Bernard Williams), Cambridge University Press, 2001, p. 193.

158 Friedrich Nietzsche, Thus Spoke Zarathustra (edited by Adrian del Caro and Robert Pippin), Cambridge University Press, 2006, p. 66 (On the Blessed Isles).

159 Ibid. p. 184.

160 Ibid. p. 9.

Already published in the same series:

Walther Ziegler
Camus in 60 Minutes
ISBN 9783741227738

Walther Ziegler
Freud in 60 Minutes
ISBN 9783741227707

Walther Ziegler
Hegel in 60 Minutes
ISBN 9783741227677

Walther Ziegler
Heidegger in 60 Minutes
ISBN 9783741227752

Walther Ziegler
Kant in 60 Minutes
ISBN 9783741226373

Walther Ziegler
Marx in 60 Minutes
ISBN 9783741227691

Walther Ziegler
Platon in 60 Minutes
ISBN 9783741227615

Walther Ziegler
Rousseau in 60 Minutes
ISBN 9783741227622

Walther Ziegler
Sartre in 60 Minutes
ISBN 9783741227653

Walther Ziegler
Smith in 60 Minutes
ISBN 9783741227721

Coming soon in the same series:

Walther Ziegler
Adorno in 60 Minutes

Walther Ziegler
Arendt in 60 Minutes

Walther Ziegler
Bacon in 60 Minutes

Walther Ziegler
Descartes in 60 Minutes

Walther Ziegler
Foucault in 60 Minutes

Walther Ziegler
Habermas in 60 Minutes

Walther Ziegler
Hobbes in 60 Minutes

Walther Ziegler
Popper in 60 Minutes

Walther Ziegler
Rawls in 60 Minutes

Walther Ziegler
Schopenhauer in 60 Minutes

Walther Ziegler
Wittgenstein in 60 Minutes

The author:

Dr Walther Ziegler is academically trained in the fields of philosophy, history and political science. As a foreign correspondent, reporter and newsroom coordinator for the German TV station ProSieben he has produced films on every continent. His news reports have won several prizes and awards.He has also authored numerous books in the field of philosophy. His many years of experience as a journalist mean that he is able to present the complex ideas of the great philosophers in a way that is both engaging and very clear. Since 2007 he has also been active as a teacher and trainer of young TV journalists in Munich, holding the post of Academic Director at the Media Academy, an institute of higher education that offers film and TV courses at its base directly on the site of the major European film production company Bavaria Film.